THE Contract

A Defined Approach on Dating/Relationships

ERNEST SMITH

Published By:
Ernest Smith
Atlanta, Georgia

www.smiththecontract.com

Designed & Produced by:
Custom Made For You
graphic design & printing studio
(770) 923-8783
www.custommadeforyou.net

Edited by Lori Hunter, Michael Finch and Sylviette McGill
Revised by Shelante Patton and Iris Flowers

ISBN Number:
978-0-615-68649-3

Notes

1. *The Bible, King James version Ephesians 5:22 and 28:31*
2. *The Bible, King James version Genesis 2:18*
3. *The Bible, King James version Corinthians 6:14*
4. *The Bible, King James version Romans 15:2*
5. *The 5 Love Languages by Gary Chapman*
6. *Wikipedia/ Encyclopedia Definitions*
7. *Urban Dictionary (reference point to definitions)*
8. *Song reference by Rocko "Go In Steady"*
9. *Allen Iverson " Talking About Practice"*
10. *Song reference Beyonce Knowles "Put a Ring On It"*
11. *Reference E.F. Hutton " When E. F. Hutton Talks People Listen"*
12. *The Bible, King James version Romans 15:2*
13. *Clint Eastwood " A Man Has Got To Know His Limitations"*
14. *Earvin "Magic" Johnson announcement he was HIV positive*

Acknowledgements

I would like to thank God for giving me the words to complete this project, without Him nothing is possible. I would like to thank everyone who supported me in purchasing this book in advance. A special thanks to those of you who supported me along the way and to all of you who participated in discussing the subject matter. I would like to thank my mother, Glenda Chandler, for all the love and support she has shown me, as well as my close friends and family.

I am dedicating this book to my late grandmother, Susie Davis, as well as to my son Darrin Smith, stepson Kobe Braynon and my grandson, Amir Smith. I would like to recognize Constance Pollard, Tosha Smith, Courtney R. Johnson and my brother, Wayne Davis, and everyone who lifted my spirit in prayer during the final days of writing this book. My brother said " I have never completed reading a book in my life, but he will read yours".

I would like to say thank you to my good friend Michael J. Finch, who was able to take my words and make them suitable for print. Last but not least, a heartfelt thank you to my first lady Vanessa J. Fuller, my number one fan, who has motivated and inspired me to complete this book.

The Contract

About the Author
Ernest D. Smith, Sr.

I was born and raised in Meridian, Miss. I now reside in Atlanta, Ga. I was raised in a single- parent home and later in my life was also a single parent after the passing of my son's mother in 1996. The idea of the "The Contract" materialized when I entered back into the dating arena following my divorce in 2008.

The issues and questions that I raise during the reading of this book were ideas that I wanted to express in a written contract, but I later realized that they would be the chapters of a book. *"For whatsoever things were written aforetime, were written for our learning, that we through patience and comfort of the scriptures might have hope."* Romans 15:2.

The Contract

Introduction

I would first like to say that this book came about as a result of an attempt to try to create a written agreement/contract, between me and anyone I met or was currently dating. The purpose of the agreement/contract, is to better communicate, meet any expectations, and determine if I was on the same page with the other person in my life. Also, it was designed with the hopes to eliminate any mind games being played, while dating. As I explored the fundamentals of dating and other social beliefs, I found a wide range of differences and expectations between men and women when it comes to dating and relationships. The differences varied based upon limited exposure to positive relationships, education, religious beliefs, geographical regions, age or the lack of a family environment. I discovered I was having the same issues as many other men in the breakdown of communication with women when it comes to dating and relationships. Following my divorce, I realized that I could only pick up where I left off regarding dating etiquette. I discovered that, as a man, adopting healthy dating mannerisms has since evolved into keeping up with dating lingo and assumptions that seem out of reach when one wants to discover the true essence of a person. Metaphorically then, dating is an undefined art of words that is based on the person's perception of how it was said but not how it was delivered.

In my agreement, I sought a mutual understanding with the person I would be dating in reference to what type of relationship we would develop. We discussed titles, our frequency of visits, the possibility of sharing expenses, our desired sexual activity, and shared interests. Curious as to how detached I was from the younger generation's thoughts regarding dating one night, I evoked conversation with Twenty-Somethings at work about their experiences, expectations, and insight. My feedback, however, was ill-received due to their lack of maturity and experience in relationships. The same question was then suggested to a mature, older generation: those in their thirties to fifties who were either divorced, single parents, or recently exited a relationship.

After reading *The Five Love Languages* by Dr. Gary Chapman, it became cathartic and assuring to know that my strength in dating and relationships pulls from my ability to offer quality time and words of affirmation to my mate. I began to reflect upon the lessons I've learned from previous failed relationships. I realized I would be destined for repeated results until I discovered what I truly wanted and desired from a woman. To better understand this, I decided to put my theory to the test and ask some of my closest female friends, as well as strangers some questions as it pertains to dating, relationships, and committed relationships to try to determine why there is an <u>adversarial</u> approach in today's society when it comes to seeking companionship. To improve in areas of open dialogue for a question and answer session to improve lines of communication, by asking the unasked questions between daters. In every aspect of our lives we have agreements or contracts; however, when it comes to our relationships with our mates there are none. From the start of boy-meets-girl relationships in grade school, written understandings have ironically set such parameters for simple encounters. For example, the all-too-well-known note requested one to check a box affirming, "Are you my boyfriend/girlfriend?" Within this paradigm, roles and limits were defined. Why then when it comes to adults, and not all, there is a mystery in what we can expect from one another. Isn't it ironic that expectations were understood with such a trite note? However, as we get older, we delve into delusion and confusion, and I ask why. Hopefully that practice of who, what, when, where, why, and how are we of dating comes to surface again. It aims to remove the guess work and the mystery. It provides a clearer understanding of who has entered my life, what this person really wants, and the ways in which I can truly be a provider. When, one might ask, is the timing right for a person to enter our lives? And too, how must we come to grips with the question of, "If not now, when?" "Where is this—and I place an emphasis on the word this—headed? And how can I measure one's genuine and true intentions? Truly, how can we earn the relationship that we mutually desire while achieving happiness as individuals and within a unit?

So then, with all this insight, this inquisitiveness, why am I single, living in the Atlanta metro area? There is a notion that the ratio of women to men exceeds great expectations. Although such common statistics may be unofficially correct, these statistics ring true to what you are looking for, willing to deal with and, in some instances, settle for. So if this can help solve some questions for those who seek monogamy, and provoke one to consider his or her actions before misleading a new partner, my authentic intent with this text would be fulfilled. One will never know what stage of life someone is in when you enter their life, I entrust my faith in the tried-and-true adage, "The one who cares the least in a relationship is the one in the greater control of the relationship." So with that being said, the focus is on a better understanding of what type of relationship you currently have, its purpose, where it is headed and what is mutually understood between the sexes. A commonly used saying states that "opposites attract," but I would ask do our differences keep us apart? Why not have an agreement during the relationship stage? There are prenuptial agreements to protect one's interests prior to marriage, and divorce settlement agreements to protect one's interests should the marriage not work. When we consider the in-between stages, the one that causes the most damage, why wouldn't a written agreement be in place?

The Contract

Table of Contents

1. Defined Relationships 13
2. Marriage 33
3. Kids 41
4. Living Arrangements 45
5. Roles 49
6. Shared Expenses 55
7. Lost Art of Dating 59
8. What is a REAL MAN? 65
9. Quality Time 69
10. Should One's Goals Be Shared? 73
11. Politics of Dating 77
12. Religion 81
13. Timing 85
14. Horoscope 91
15. Technology and Dating 93
16. Temptation or Cheating 99
17. A Discussion on One's Sexual History 105
18. Income 115
19. Loans or Gifts 121
20. Pets 125
21. Background Checks and Drug Test 127
22. An Agreement on Physical Appearance 131
23. Ethics and Morals 135
24. Why Am I Single? 143
25. Synopsis 147
26. Glossary 151

The Contract

Defined Relationship
(Friend, Dating, Relationship, Committed Relationship)

Friend: is a person attached to another by feelings of affection or personal regard, a person who gives assistance; a patron; supporter, a person who is on good terms with another, a person who is not hostile.

When I entered back into the dating ranks, I've come to learn that the word friend as stated: "a friend or commonly my friend," is strongly mistaken and out of its proper passage. To put it into proper prospective as it relates to dating and relationships, a friend is a person who has periodic attachment at certain times, with mixed feelings, whom you may or may not support depending on certain events and circumstances, and on good terms the majority of times with good understandings. Friend sometimes has a close meaning to the following lingo words like companion, my sponsor, my boo, cut buddy, jump off, freak, home boy/ girl and is associated with the phrases "friends with benefits", "booty call", and the most popular, "we just kicking it".

Dating is derived from the word date. During the process of dating, you can date multiple individuals, on social appointments and engagements, or occasion beforehand that may or may not lead to a relationship.

As the word dating is defined in today's world, it is misrepresented and quite often confused with the word relationship. When someone thinks the person they are dating is exclusive to them and only them, should the questions arise? "Are you dating someone else or multiple people"? Since dating may lead or may not lead to a relationship. In most cases this is the exit point and one may be downgraded to the word "friend", the street term, of course.

The term serial dater was derived from a person having multiple dates daily or several weekly with no clear purpose or focus; only to secure some type of desired gain. This individual sometimes impedes the dating process and causes great disruption of individuals seeking true intent in the dating process.

Relationship: a connection, association, or involvement between persons by blood or marriage, an emotional or another connection between people, an involvement or a sexual affair.

This definition is the easiest of the four due to fact that relationship is derived from dating. It's a graduate program in most cases; however, it can also be confusing due to the relationship that must be fully spelled out by asking key questions in the communication breakdown, such as, "Is this only a sexual relationship?" "How often will you interact?" "What type of activities will we be doing?", or "Is it exclusive?" "And what are the expectations?" Some close knit words associated with the lingo definition are "my companion", "my man/woman", "my lady", and the certain "we go together".

Committed relationship: An interpersonal bond based upon a mutually agreed-upon commitment to one another involving exclusivity, honesty and openness. Some examples of committed relationships include close friendship, courtship, long-term relationships, engagement, marriage, and civil unions.

This is the most serious of all defined relationships and is one step shy of marriage; and the problem in the majority of all relationships is, due to the word "commit". Commit means to put in trust or in charge. The majority of committed relationships are long term, with rings being exchanged with the intent of marriage, the majority leading to living together (shacking up) where one has more access to one another and shared expenses of living is involved; however, this relationship even though one would think is monogamous may not be in all circumstances. Closely related lingos in this instance would be again my "man", "lady", or "my significant other".

Now that I have defined all four current scenarios which one are you currently in? Which one does your mate think you are currently in based on the definitions in both dictionary and in society? Do you need a mutual agreement/ contract based upon answers?

Below are some questions to ask during the process of dating to help develop or identify your stage.

1. Did the above define guideline raise issues of what stage you are currently in a dating/ relationship?
❑ Yes
❑ No

2.Does having sexual relations with someone you are dating constitute a relationship?
❑ Yes
❑ No

3.Should you reveal to someone that you are dating that you are sexually active with someone else that you are also dating?
❑ Yes
❑ No

4.In the interest of not wasting time, should pre-established time frames be set to determine the progression of the relationship? For example: In 6 months I expect to be dating someone exclusively and in two years I expect to be engaged.
❑ Yes
❑ No

5.During the dating phase, should women also be expected to pay for some dates?
❑ Yes
❑ No

I couldn't fully discuss the above information without fully exploring the issue of deal breakers identified from both men and women during the initial stages of meeting someone, dating, and committed relationships that could make the above process interchangeable.

Deal Breakers upon First Meeting a Man

- Late more than 30 minutes with no follow-up or explanation
- Rude
- No manners or gentleman qualities
- Bad teeth and/or breath (poor hygiene) appearance
- Coming onto me too strong (trying to touch me, making inappropriate or sexual comments about my body, trying to kiss me when it's not reciprocated)
- Quiet or shy and has a hard time holding a conversation or poor communication
- Incompatible
- Money issues or not stable
- Smoker or Drinking Issues
- No physical attraction
- Being Cocky or Arrogant
- No relationship with God
- No goals or aspirations
- Has children but no active role in their lives, support, etc.
- Poor grammar
- No car
- Already in a relationship

The Contract

Deal Breakers While Dating

- Flirting with other women while with me, whether it is blatant or down low
- Having the expectation that he can date other women, but getting upset if I do the same and date others
- Inconsiderate of my time and family obligations (i.e. kids) or poor manners
- Wants children
- Abusive (mental, verbal and/or physical)
- Lack of communication
- Mistrust or a Liar
- Sex issues
- He still lives at home or not having his own place
- He talks bad about his ex or baggage
- Always insist at being at your place
- Interest in sex only as it appears he isn't genuine in getting to know you
- No goals, purpose
- Never do any activities sit around the house
- Selfish
- No affection
- No gentleman like qualities (door open)
- Does not attend any church services

The Contract

Deal Breakers while in Relationship

- Unwillingness to accept my children
- Lack of trust
- Poor communication
- Different perspective and expectation of relationship
- Infidelity/ cheating
- Emotional, physical, or mental abuse
- He never invites you to his residence
- No quality time
- Always hanging out with the fellows/ club scene
- Not romantic / spontaneous
- Unstable / Lack of finances
- Insecure
- No personal goals/ Not supportive
- Uncircumcised
- No talk of shared dreams/ future
- Have not met each other's family
- Intimate connection or sexual dysfunctions
- Penis size

The Contract

Deal Breakers in a Committed Relationship

- No communication

- Never talk of marriage

- No ring

- Still playing games

- Insecure

- Not supportive

- Infidelity / Cheating

- Signs of abuse: emotional, mental and physical

The Contract

Deal Breakers upon First Meeting a Woman

- Asking to pay their bills
- Kids by multiple men
- Appearance/ gold or bad teeth, facial piercings, multiple visual tattoos, dirty nails
- Poor grammar
- No lady like qualities
- Drinks to excess
- Dress inappropriately
- Facial Hair
- Physical Appearance, Not In Shape
- Still Married or not actually single
- Smoker
- Bad Breath

The Contract

Top Deal Breakers when Dating a Woman

- No affection

- Lies

- Needy or complaining always a victim

- No goals

- Always clubbing with her girlfriends

- Expects more from others than she does of herself

- Un-behaved kids

- Never offers to pay during the dating phase

- Disrespectful or loud

- Can't laugh and relax

- Drunk or Drug User

- Has body Odor or Bad breath

- Bringing children on date

- Late

The Contract

Top Deal Breakers While in Relationship

- Lies
- Cheats
- Always hanging with girlfriends
- Never cooks
- No affection
- No job or career
- Thief
- Non- Christian
- Superficial or worried what others think
- Take for granted and unappreciated

The Contract

Top Ways to Identify That You are in a Committed Relationship

- Proposal of Marriage

- Living Together

- Getting Engaged (different from proposal of marriage)

- Making major purchases (house, car, land)

The Contract

Marriage

Growing up in the late 1960's, I learned through watching my older aunts and uncles that marriage was forever and marriage vows were "until death do us part." In today's world of a 50% divorce rate, myself included, the question was did I really want to get married again? If I was to meet someone and that was a priority in her life, would I actually be wasting her time if I didn't want to get married? With my uncertainty of exactly what I wanted at that stage in my life, it would have been wrong for me to enter into a relationship where I put my self-serving interest above the goals of another person. One in five adults ages 25 and older have never been married. What I've discovered is that there are a lot of people dating, in relationships, and in committed relationships where one partner actually has no idea the other doesn't want to get married which I feel is a result of poor <u>communication</u>. If this subject was discussed in the beginning stages and not pushed to the side, and there was an <u>agreement/ contract</u> up front, I wondered if there would be more or less couples entering into committed relationships? The answers or reasons may be endless, but again, my main idea was to ask from the very beginning do you plan on getting married? With this simple question, a lot of time could be saved and the relationship could be redefined.

If you find yourself in a relationship/ committed relationship with no clear sign of marriage, maybe some type of agreement or contract should be an option. In some situations, the pressures associated with dating and relationships from friends, family, society and biological clocks could lead to someone seeking a committed relationship when they're truly not ready for one. Or it could lead to passing on certain individuals in hopes of finding one that is better. During my research, I came across an attractive 30 year-old female, when I inquired as to her status, she stated she was currently in a relationship with her man for 27 months. I asked her why she referenced the exact number of months of the relationship? She stated, "Well, I'm a woman, we count everything." I asked if they were currently living together and she replied "no" and that she hoped to be engaged within the next year. I verified that she said, "hope to be engaged." She confirmed, "Yes." So, I asked if she still considered herself to be in a committed relationship or just a relationship. As I walked away, the look on her face was priceless. I, being a total stranger, brought to her attention the time already invested and future time that would be invested without a clear agreement. So, if you are taking the time to be exact on the number of months in detail, then why not take the time to fully discuss the future on paper? This is just one example of how the lack of a clear agreement within a time frame, in relation to marriage, can be an issue of whether or not nuptials will take. One word that is used in today's relationship world is <u>ultimatum</u>, the situation is a case where one party dictates his or her needs in a relationship, which is far more unpleasant than an agreement/contract that is negotiated by both parties on equal terms. Many couples have failed to understand that marriage is what comes after the wedding and all of the planning associated with the wedding: from who's in the wedding, where the occasion will take place, to who will or won't be invited, the seating chart, the honeymoon, and the gifts. Following the ceremony is when the real work comes in, and that is the work of applying and living within the covenants of marriage. As I have learned, this would be one of the hardest, but most fulfilling jobs on earth! Each day brings a different challenge, but the reward, if accomplished, is priceless.

When I opened the dialogue about marriage with men, the major issue I heard over and over again was that women don't know how to be submissive or submit unto a man. So the first thing I must do is fully define what it means to submit or to be in submission. *"Submitting yourselves one to another in the fear of God. Wives, submit yourselves unto*

your own husbands, as the Lord, for the husband is the head of the wife,
even as Christ is the head of the church", according to Ephesians 5:21-23.
Often, many of us take passages from the Bible out of context, or to
serve it in a context just to benefit ourselves; however, I can relate to
the men in this situation. Unfortunately, one of the downfalls of my
marriage was that even though my now ex-wife was an avid church-
goer, she never fully submitted to me. This was the topic of conversation one weekend when she called me from a women's church retreat.
She actually apologized to me for her past behavior. She stated that
after learning and discussing this subject with the older members
of the church, she realized that my role in the family was not truly
defined. Upon her return from the retreat, for three consecutive days
I had a fully submissive wife. Shortly thereafter, things were back to
normal and traits of the independent woman had resurfaced. Feeling that I had somehow failed, I sought the advice of my aunt, who
had remained married for 45 years until her husband passed away
in 1998. She explained that although there was love, respect, and
chemistry that existed between my wife and me, it was the possibility the thing we were missing was the principle of not being equally
yoked. As I pondered, I thought back to some of our differences and
why we grew apart. Things such as attending church together and
listening to the same sermon, even though our interpretations of it
were much different, were some of the reasons. With my southern
upbringing and southern roots, I valued saving and providing. She,
being from the big city, loved spending and living life to the fullest.
I knew this going into the marriage, but like most, I thought she
would change in her thought process with marriage. I would like to
say that although the marriage did not survive, we ended the relationship with class and dignity, just as we started. To this day, we are
business partners and communicate on different levels of our newly
defined friendship.

Challenges Associated With Planning a Wedding

Issues can arise when planning a wedding and trying to finalize the
wedding party. In one of my case studies; the bride-to-be had great
objection to one of the groomsmen selection. It was believed that the

symbol of marriage would have been tarnished had the chosen person remained because of the fact that the person who was selected had been having an affair for the past six years. After a lengthy conversation, a mutual agreement was reached removing this individual from the wedding party.

Now the discussion of the ring; from all the conversations regarding the cost associated with it to the size of the diamond. We can't continue fully without defining what the symbol of the ring means due to similar ideas were lost with the wedding, in such that so much is planned that the afterthought of the marriage has been lost. For example, the size of the wedding, who pays, and who's invited or not invited. Questions arise from whether it's one's first wedding or not, will it be a traditional wedding, or straight to the courthouse? These issues come to the forefront during the planning stages and maybe if a mutual agreement of past discussions was in place, maybe it could have resolved any and/ or all problems. It is well recognized that the cost of the ring is based on three months of the man's salary, with this the only issue whether it, is in the reference to the net or the gross income? The issues of the ring amount pertain to the size, clarity, and yes, the cost. So what are the compromises? In one instance I've learned that the engagement was actually called off due to the size and cost of the ring. So let's define the ring and what it symbolizes. Conventionally, the woman's ring is presented as a betrothal gift by a man to his prospective spouse while he proposes marriage or directly after she accepts his marriage proposal. It represents a formal agreement to future marriage. So with this information we will explore several below questions regarding the engagement/wedding ring. In another instance, I learned that the actual engagement was called off due to the fact that no clear agreement could be reached in reference to the cost of the ring. The potential bride's girlfriends insisted that the ring should be a certain carat size while the potential groom was old school and went with traditional values of thinking of associated costs. This brings me to another major question: if the wedding does not commence and is canceled, is the ring to be returned to the groom? Many women will not like the answer, as I have researched and according to laws of the state you reside in, the ring is considered a gift with the contemplation of marriage which is a contract/ agreement. If no wedding takes place, the gift of the ring should be returned back to the man. In this case maybe a compromise of an agreement could have been reached. For example, maybe on a certain anniversary, the size of the carat of the ring could have been upgraded; however, if the issue of the ring was the problem and not the focus of the marriage, would there have been an anniversary to upgrade on?

The wedding: a ceremony in which two people are united in marriage of Holy Matrimony or a similar institution. Wedding traditions and customs vary greatly between cultures, ethnic groups, religions, countries, and social classes. Most wedding ceremonies involve an exchange of wedding vows by the couple, presentation of a gift, ring offering, symbolic item, flowers, money and a public proclamation of marriage by an authority figure or leader. Special wedding garments are often worn, and the ceremony is sometimes followed by a wedding reception. Music, poetry, prayers or readings from religious texts or literature are also commonly incorporated into the ceremony. It was tradition that all cost associated with a wedding is at the expense of the bride's family with the groom's family paying for the rehearsal dinner. If this is understood, all is well. Several questions could arise if there were no prior discussions or agreements confirmed in this area. Some couples elect to elope, go to the courthouse, or in some cases have a small wedding with a select group of family and friends. Whatever the case, questions are raised in the subjects of marriage, wedding, and the ring.

Here are some commonly ask questions that were brought to my attention.

1.If he or she is over a certain age say (40) and has never married or has no kids is this a possible red flag?
❑ Yes
❑ No

2.Should marriage traditions associated with the cost of a wedding ring still be that of 3 months of a man's salary?
❑ Yes
❑ No

3.If it is a man's second wedding should the cost of the second ring be greater than that of the prior marriage?
❑ Yes
❑ No

4.If the bride's parents are deceased or it is her second wedding should the groom and bride split the cost of the wedding?
❑ Yes
❑ No

5.Should the words obey be included in the wedding vows for the bride to recite?
❑ Yes
❑ No

6.Is it a red flag if a person has been married and divorced at least three times?
❑ Yes
❑ No

7.Should a woman submit or be submissive to her husband during the course of the marriage?

❑ Yes

❑ No

8.In the event that the wedding does not take place should the woman return the engagement ring to the man?

❑ Yes

❑ No

9.Should couples live together prior to marriage in order to experience one's living habits?

❑ Yes

❑ No

10. Should a husband or wife have friends of the opposite sex outside of their shared friends?

❑ Yes

❑ No

11. Would you ask the person that you were engaged to for a prenuptial agreement?

❑ Yes

❑ No

12. Should couples that lived together have a fresh start by buying new furniture, so there won't be any past history of prior relationships?

❑ Yes

❑ No

The Contract

Kids

I remember the old childhood chant that rings, "Jack and Jill sitting in a tree <u>K-I-S-S-I-N-G</u> /first comes love/ then comes marriage/ here comes Jack pushing the baby carriage." Really? After marriage and reaching a certain age, I've come to the honest conclusion that I really don't want any more kids. I have met and dated several women where they have stressed a strong desire of wanting kids in the future. I must be honest; I may have been <u>selfish</u> as I put my desires before theirs and their ultimate goal of childbirth due to the fact that I was in their life <u>in the meantime</u>. So I performed an honest self-assessment and understood that I wasn't being fair to the other person at the time (or anyone in the future) by not expressing my intent not to have additional children. I talked with several former married couples and asked what if they would share the reason for their breakup? I was told that the spouse didn't want to have kids. I asked them whether or not they had discussed the topic during the dating and <u>courtship</u> phase of the relationship and I received several different responses. One stated that he/ she did want kids, but did not tell the other person prior to marriage that their thoughts had changed. That individual didn't think the other was serious upon the initial discussion and that he/ she would not eventually get married.

The most common answer was that he/ she changed their mind due to selfish reasons or thought he/ she could <u>change</u> the other person's mind. The latter seems to be a common goal in marriage talks. Somehow people think they can change their partners' mind. It almost never happens. There are always exceptions.

So ask when meeting someone, in a respectful way would you like to have children in the future?

❑ Yes
❑ No

Time is of the essence, depending upon one's age and biological clock and having some type of mutual agreement could save time, energy, and great disappointment.

While working out in the gym about four years ago, an attractive lady in her late forties inquired if I knew a good workout routine to remove some weight due to the birth of her youngest child two years prior. As I recommended ideas to her she further explained her thought process for having a child at such a late stage in her life. She stated that her husband was previously married and had adult children and when they met the topic of children was not of major concern to the relationship as both had fully raised their respective children to maturity. When they married, she expressed the desire to have one additional child with him. She had an adult child from a previous relationship, yet she still yearned for one additional child as she had put off having children so that she may accomplish other goals. She explained that this was not receptive to him and after months of him refraining from sex due to this subject, he finally gave in. During the conclusion of my workout, I was able to meet her beautiful daughter which she further noted was a "daddy's girl." Through the art of reaching an agreement on this subject, their marriage was on an even stronger foundation. As I said, there are always exceptions.

1.Would you continue dating someone if you were fully aware that he/she wanted kids and they fully expected that you were seeking the same but you felt differently?

❑ Yes

❑ No

2.If you changed your mind from initially wanting kids in the future, to not wanting them but was in a happy relationship/ committed relationship would you tell your mate?

❑ Yes

❑ No

3.Should one divulge that he/she has had a vasectomy or a tubal ligation during the dating stage if one is seeking children from the onset of the conversation?

❑ Yes

❑ No

4.Would you ever consider adoption as an alternative to having kids while in a committed relationship?

❑ Yes

❑ No

5.While married or in a committed relationship in the event one party should change their mind or view point on additional kids in the household is it of great importance to the other individual or spouse?

❑ Yes

❑ No

The Contract

Living Arrangements

One would think that living together would be a prerequisite to marriage. This is a way of learning more about one's living habits prior to marriage, and a better way of getting use to your future spouse. In my survey, I learned that some couples have lived together for years, and in some cases decades, and they have yet to make the final commitment of marriage.

First, I would like to discuss the benefits of living together, then the expectations, the financial breakdown, and the effects if it is a failure.

As I first explained the theory of a contract with a much younger generation, it generated much excitement. I found that many young couples, after the completion of high school, were eager to cohabitate from under their parent's roof and rules. As I tried to explain potential problems of cohabitation, they were quickly dismissed; so that's why I will focus on the mature generation. It is assumed that living together will be a financial benefit or a plus for both. However, the majority of individuals in this agreement actually tend to take on more debt during the course of the relationship.

The following are some major issues:
If a man and woman live together without the covenant of marriage, how will the living expenses be shared? Would the same expectations be the same or would they change if the same couple were married? Some of the issues that arose were who would be responsible for what? If one party were to become unemployed,

would the other party assume the additional responsibility? If so, one must then ask for how long? Would there be time given for the other party to gain employment?

Below is a breakdown of some of the living arrangements.

Is a man responsible for all the financial bills of the household?
❑ Yes
❑ No

Is a man responsible for half of all bills in the household?
❑ Yes
❑ No

Should the man be responsible for the mortgage or rent, and the woman be responsible for utilities?
❑ Yes
❑ No

Now some of the individuals I spoke to somewhat referenced the Bible for some of their guidance in reference to how they came to their decision. The irony is, they referenced passages in the Bible that pertained to married couples. According to Ephesians 5:22 and 28-31, the position of the husband in the home and his related responsibilities are quite clearly defined in principle. *"Wives submit yourselves unto your husband, as unto the Lord. For the husband is the head of the wife, even as Christ is the head of the church; and He is the savior of the body. Therefore, the church is subject to Christ, so let wives be subject to their own husbands in everything. Husbands love your wife as Christ also loved the church and gave himself for it. So ought men to love their wives as their own bodies." "He that loveth his wife loveth himself. For no man ever yet hated his own flesh but nourisheth and cherisheth it, even as the Lord the church. For this cause shall a man leave his father and mother and shall be joined unto his wife, and they two shall be one flesh"*.

The second reference was from the Bible, Genesis 2:18:
"And the Lord God said "it is not good that the man should be alone; I will make him a help mate for him."

Finally, if there are kids in the household, then should the rent be divided equally by the number of occupants and the biological parent of the minor is covered by that parent?

These were the top four responses to my question, so prior to moving in with that special person, please ask and explore the appropriate questions and answers. The majority of the logic I received was from references found in the Bible, such as, should a man pay for all living expenses even though the couple is not married? However, during the second and more popular study, the answer appeared to be an understanding that all living arrangements and expenses should be shared. The third study was also a reference from the Bible stating a woman's role should be a help mate. The fourth answer that was recorded was valid; however but was in the minority due to there was a strong disagreement as I discussed this idea with couples. I too have some difficulties as it pertains to this subject. It is my personal belief that if I am to enter into a committed relationship and were to respectfully request that she move in with me, there wouldn't be any issue of me providing for the household at the current time or in the future. So this would assure her of any future questions that may arise if there ever was a proposal of marriage.

The Contract

Roles

In cohabitating, there were several issues and concerns that were identified regarding roles within the home. For example, how would the responsibilities of cooking, cleaning, maintenance, and disciplining of children be addressed? The major question in this aspect was whether or not a non-biological person in the relationship discipline the minor children. How would issues with former ex's or former spouses be resolved? There are many concerns in this area that will persist long after this book has ended. Most feel that if a child is living under their roof, and that person is the authoritarian and that the house rules have been established, any punishments set should be enforced. Is corporal punishment by the non-biological parent permissible? Would you allow the person you are currently in a relationship with to discipline your child? Would the non-custodial biological father or mother object and would this cause a great disruption in the household?

I will not offer my opinion on the matter but I will offer my experience having been on both sides of the equation. My son's mom married when he was eight and I met the step-father in passing prior to the marriage. There was very little that was discussed between us. However, knowing my son's mom from the age of 12 and having a solid foundation with her, I trusted her judgment that anyone she brought around my son and eventually married would be a positive influence on my son. One of the issues that I did have a problem with was how he was to be addressed... meaning would my son address him by his name or would he be called dad? To answer the first question, I didn't have a problem with my son being disciplined by another man as long as it was warranted and his mother was well informed. Again, as the head of the household, all of his rules that were set as a family must be followed and whatever discipline was set as punishment had to be carried out in raising him in the family unit. My case may be unique because there was never a need, while my son's mom was alive for him ever to resort to corporal punishment in my son's case. The way the issue of how he would be addressed was left up to my son and his comfort level with his step dad. There were very few issues thereafter. The reason I left it up to him was because I was secure in my relationship and role in my son's life. I was an active father and provider and he knew I loved him. On the opposite side of the equation, when I married and became a stepfather, there were issues in the disciplining of my stepson. In this case, his father objected to the idea of me ever being put in that position, due to her job with the airlines and her absence from the home at the time of the occurrence of misbehavior. This may have been as a result of poor interaction between us from the onset and trust as we had our trials and tribulation in the early years. Looking back on the situation, I must say I was more at fault, say 60/40, in how those encounters were handled. In the end, I think in all cases we both agreed the more the child is loved by the masses the more the child will thrive as it relates to the old African proverb "It takes a village to raise a child".

After the breakup of my marriage, there came a time when my stepson's father made sure I was active in his life. I was involved in a new relationship with a woman who had a son of her own. After having my stepson for the weekend, I received a call from his father. He stressed an issue that arose during my stepson's visit with me pertaining to my new relationship interest and her son. My stepson was upset and thought that if I was to start a new family that I would not have time for him and that her son was somewhat of a replacement. After reassuring that this would never take place, I thanked his father for the call and to this day all interaction between us has been on a positive and mutually respectful level. I can say we are now friends and when I hear the phrase <u>real man</u>, I actually think of my stepson's father. Because of the level of respect between us, there have been many occasions of interaction including,the funeral of my former mother-in-law, where we both rode in a family limousine with our son and later he drove me to the airport. Interactions in a positive tone from the very beginning will last and benefit all parties involved.

While living together other issues are brought to the fore front such as personal hygiene, cleanliness, cooking, lawn maintenance, one coming home at inappropriate times or not coming home at all. If these areas are not fully discussed there will be serious problems causing the demise of the relationship. During interviews with several former couples, information was obtained and so much was learned in the process. A drawback to the shared expense philosophy is sometimes you tend to go into additional debt thinking that you save money but tend to make more major purchases that increase your debt ratio. This is the ultimate cause of many couples learning how to get together but not knowing fully how to end the relationship due to financial obligations will keep you together. If all of this comes after you get together then how and when do you break up? It was brought to my attention and it happens in some marriages, that there have been agreements due to financial obligations that couples remained together because they couldn't afford to live apart. Due to a codependency of comingled funds this causes great turmoil and further expectations are sometimes demanded. The basic question is, would a mutual agreement/ contract resolve some of, if not all, of these issues? Some elect to remain due to the depression, insecurities, and the uncertainties of life and what it has to offer, meaning you've become dependent on that one person and you're no longer whole when you are divided. The singles I interviewed stated that they were somewhat afraid to move on or didn't know how to start the process and may continue to invest time and energy in a bad relationship because they are afraid to start fresh.

When dating and pursuing a relationship do you look first at the person as a good individual for your family as it pertains to your children and in the interest of your needs first? As this relates to parenting and the interaction of the noncustodial parent, there could be issues. The questions of what stage of the relationship should one meet the children? As well as what stage should he/ she meet the noncustodial parent, due to the fact that person will be spending a great deal of time with the child or children?

As in marriages, there will be disagreements and conflicts that arise and some seek the advice of others, maybe family or friends. Should both parties agree not to allow the input of others and continue to reach a mutual understanding between themselves? But, when involving others, some of the drawbacks are selfserving of one's advice to one member of the couple and this could cause conflict. I would say please find a person that is neutral or a mediator of sorts that would be opened minded about the subject matter of discussion. I suggest anyone who is not emotionally involved in your lives which could include individuals such as a pastor or counselor. This agreement could also be used to identify possible family and friends that ask for help via living assistance or actually reside in your home. Some parameters' should be identified beforehand.

Some of the people you reach out to may have a self- serving interest, meaning there may be an alternative motive in their advice. Some may have hidden agendas, such as jealousy, envy, or may in some ways want to emulate your life. The age-old saying "misery does love company" proves to be true. When I was growing up, I heard the following expressions: "Show me your friends and I will show you your future" and "Family will bring you down quicker than anything else." In regard to these two statements, would you honor their opinion and judgment on who you should be dating and/or in a relationship with? One rule of thought, if you don't want them in your business then please don't discuss private matters or your personal life. One of the major issues I've observed in the course of my life is the interference of family members and friends offering some sort of unsolicited advice on your life. To keep this aspect out of your life, please discuss with the person you are dating and in a relationship with some type of agreement that when there are issues he or she won't have to entertain the thought of some people interjecting their thought or beliefs unto you.

1.Should the nonparent boyfriend or girlfriend discipline the child of another?

❑ Yes
❑ No

2.Should introductions be a priority between couples that are just dating and the ex's of the children to fully communicate who is interacting around the children to possibly eliminate issues that may arise in the future?

❑ Yes
❑ No

3.Is a man considered the head of the household in a committed relationship if he is not paying the majority of the bills?

❑ Yes
❑ No

4.Is it appropriate for minor children to address the non-parent as mama or daddy?

❑ Yes
❑ No

5. In the event of a relationship becoming serious should there be some type of mutual agreement to ensure that the noncustodial parent, is fully aware by meeting a prospective person for his or her child's welfare so that all concerns are not an issue?

❑ Yes
❑ No

6.Should a mutual agreement or contract be specified excluding family members or friends from the interference of the relationship?

❑ Yes
❑ No

7.What is the agreed upon rule of expectancy for a child who matures into an adult moving out of the house?

❑ Never

❑ When the child is financially able

❑ At age ____ if the child is not in school full time

8.Should there be a written agreement or contingency with firm stipulations should family members and friends of the time frame of their stay, their financial & household while in your home?

❑ Yes

❑ No

9.Should there be a mutual agreement in case the relationship ends and alternate living arrangements must be made/ meaning a clear understanding of a backup plan and it be followed?

❑ Yes

❑ No

10. When moving into your partner's residence, should there be a discussion of being added to the deed?

❑ Yes

❑ No

11. When do you begin sharing a bank account/ finances with your partner and would you have a hidden account?

❑ Yes

❑ No

Shared Expenses

Growing up in Meridian, Mississippi, and dating in the mid-1980s, chivalry and courtship were highly regarded. Those were the times when a young man would walk a young lady home, ask her to the prom, sit on the porch with her until reaching curfew and maybe if lucky get a kiss. The good old days! As it relates to expenses, it was expected that a young man would pay the bill of any expenses associated with dating to include prom, movies, sporting events, dances, etc. This came with the clear expectation that he/she was the only one the individual was currently dating or in a relationship with. Time was limited between school, work and daily chores that dating was a bonus or perk. As I got older, it occurred to me that dating is just that, a game! It is often a guessing game of am I the only one she is dating, to how much should I spend, and will the night end in sexual intercourse.

One major issue for me is when did the word date or going on a date mean the same as going out to eat? This concept is prevalent in today's dating world and has caused great confusion. Where is the <u>art of planning</u> a date such as a picnic in the park? A story was told to me once that the best date a woman had ever been on was with a man that had very limited <u>funds</u> because he went to the finest details of organizing the picnic basket from napkins, to straws, to food items and beverages. It was the thought that he had put in the planning stage that captured her heart. I've learned that there are many activities to do other than eating; such as, walking, working out, or meeting at a coffee shop, that's never explored. Dating in today's economy is an <u>investment</u>. So how do we date? What I have learned from some women is that conversation far outweighs a free meal any day and most would opt for a coffee shop or park as long as it's in a quiet setting and not going to one's house on the first encounter.

There was a lost dating fundamental back in the day called going <u>Dutch</u>. The idea is that each party paid for his/ her own meals so there was no misunderstanding of intentions. If there was no mutual attraction for the future, they went on their separate ways. Today's theory from the majority of women is clear that a man should pay on the first date, IF NOT ALL DATES. My objective here is to come to an understanding of what each person is thinking while on the first date. This may cloud one's judgment and leading to some future errors. So we must first define <u>date</u> before proceeding. Secondly, we must identify the objective for the date. Finally, at the conclusion of the date, hopefully it would be clearly communicated if there is a mutual attraction and a desire for continued contact. A few issues arise in dating, one, when we ask ourselves afterwards, is the person we just met, his/ her <u>representative</u> or is this a possible <u>serial dater</u> which will mislead one in their true intentions.

This brings to mind something that happened a couple of years ago, while dining at a popular food chain restaurant. The restaurant had a "buy one entrée and get the second at no charge" promotion. The way I looked at it was like most men, "no harm no foul". So, in theory, if I didn't like her the meal was free, and if I did like her my meal was free. So I ask, where are those specials today, when they are drastically needed? This was the major issue during the interaction with both sexes, and I will put both viewpoints out to hopefully clarify things from both sides. No romance without finance and exclusivity were two of the major issues in the dating stage. Men felt as if they were doing what was expected as men as in wining and dining. Why isn't that enough? It seemed that women required more and would not oblige without things being clearly defined as exclusive. The next issue was if there was no romance why should the financing be continued only by one party and should the endeavor of future dates be shared?

Below are some of the questions from both sexes that were raised during dating, relationships, and committed relationships.

1.When a man asks a woman to meet for drinks what is he asking?
❑Drinks only
❑Food included

2.What is the ideal first date?
❑Meeting at a coffee shop
❑Meeting at a park
❑Meet at a restaurant for lunch or dinner
❑Other

3.If a woman asks a man out on a date should she pay?
❑ Yes
❑ No

4.Is a man required to offer for the upkeep of a woman's hair, nails, etc. while dating?
❑ Yes
❑ No

5.On a first date, how long should one wait at the destination if you have not heard from the other person?
❑30 minutes
❑45 minutes
❑1 hour

6.Should women be sensitive on first dates to men when ordering food items and drinks as it relates to the check?
❑ Yes
❑ No

7.When was the last time a woman cooked a home cooked meal for you?
❑One week
❑One month
❑More than a two months

8. This question is for men, have you ever thought while on a date would she have ordered that meal or number of drinks if she was paying for it?
❏ Yes
❏ No

9. Would you look differently at a person if he or she used a coupon on a date or took you to a restaurant that was having a special on entrees that were two for one?
❏ Yes
❏ No

10. Do men really think it's a turn off when women have expectations for you to purchase drinks while in a night club or bar?
❏ Yes
❏ No

11. While dating is there such a thing as a sexual side of the menu or a price amount that expectations would require sexual activity?
❏ Yes
❏ No

12. While dating is it appropriate to ask for any type of financial support whether it is for mortgage, rent, or car (to include gas) payments?
❏ Yes
❏ No

13. During the dating process is it polite or courteous for women to pay for every other date or if a man pays for dinner for the woman to offer to pay for a movie, as an example?
❏ Yes
❏ No

Lost Art of Dating

As "date or dating" was defined earlier, we never identified the purpose or reason one would put him or her through emotional trials and tribulations and the pain and suffering that sometimes are the ending consequences. To remain positive, we all want and need to be loved and share life's experiences with someone that we are <u>equally yoked</u> with. There is an old saying you have to kiss a few frogs to find that one prince. For us men how much do you have to spend to find that princess? Honestly, is it worth it?

Some people along the way will show no honesty, loyalty, integrity, courage, and fidelity. The rewards may in some cases far exceed the down falls in finding a husband or wife, a best friend, experiencing birth of children and one true soul mate. No one really wants to truly grow old and alone. I've asked myself why older people would marry one another if there is limited activity due to physical limitations. Then it hit me! It was the time that they spent together conversing of the wisdom and knowledge gained through the art of positive and continued communication and the sharing of dreams that bonded them together. The challenge for anyone who reads this book is to live, share, and not waste the time of others because the true time eventually wasted is one's own.

My hope is to discuss the issues of dating in our community. I see very few articles in the press about other races and their difficulties in the dating process. Allen Iverson once stated, "we are talking about practice", and here we are talking about dating— the lost fundamentals of an old, forgotten art. The words I learned early on were gentleman, lady like, etiquette; and chivalry. For some, I must define them due to the issues we all are experiencing, causing us to sometimes forget why we are actually dating. For some it's become an insane process, and I know I am not the only one who is shaking my head because of the stories I have heard from others.

We must not forget what we are trying to accomplish in the process of dating. The objective is to meet and learn more about one another and not focus so much on the idea of where we are going and what can I eat or get? Let the conversation be on each other: allowing each to express their wants, their needs, their desires, and their goals; and let's be conscious of the other person's time, energy and sacrifices that it takes to accomplish on arriving on time. Let's not forget the respect of being on time or if running late showing the respect and courtesy of calling to fully explain a change in plan, time, or cancellation. Be mindful and courteous of the person you are meeting when ordering from the menu. Ask yourself would you have ordered that if you were paying for it? At the end of the date, don't mislead the other person. Fully communicate to your date any intentions of a second encounter. Don't say things such as you will call if you have no intention of calling. If you took the time and energy to meet the person in the first place, take a little extra time, and have the class to be honest concerning your future intent.

In some scenarios, if one person was not attracted to the other or some expectations were not met in some dating criteria, certain exit strategies would come into play. Remember, the only dumb question is the one not asked. Therefore, if you are attracted to me just ask, do I appear to be your type? During this process, take the time to ascertain information that can aid you in learning about pros and cons pertaining to yourself. One forgets dating is about gaining knowledge, and in some cases networking, and if all else fails gaining a friend. Women often ask me where chivalry went. The answers I received from men were it was dead because women killed it. There is no rule book for men or women and hopefully this could be a determination of how to better communicate, remembering that each person is an individual and unique like fingerprints. No one is the same and what you do for one person may not work for the next. For example, when it comes to dating etiquette, a man can do the same exact thing for what one woman who may have thought it was ideal but the next might consider it to be a deal breaker. So how do we get pass this stage is the question? I went out on a date once and was sitting there waiting for her arrival. My date approached the table and I stood up; her immediate reaction was, obviously, to ask why. I explained that I was taught it was customary for a man to rise when a lady approached. To take this one step further, a man can make this a practice nine out of ten times, but the one time that he fails to do such action, he will be called out and therefore looked at in a different way in her eyes and not that of a <u>gentleman</u>.

How is a <u>real man</u> defined through the eyes of a woman? This is a very touchy subject with men because women have never walked in the shoes of men, and when you add the issues associated with being a man, which are often difficult to describe, it gets even harder to clearly define. Men only wish not to use such a derogatory tone in reference to where it should fully be applied. In my relationship with women, this question is closely related to how the man will provide, the relationship he has with his kids and the quality time he has with them. Whether he maintains a job and if unemployed, is he always actively seeking one? Does he have goals and aspirations? Is he loyal, responsible and able to admit when he is wrong, as well as treating a woman like she should be treated? But most importantly, does he honor God as the foundation of his life? These are just a few attributes women look for when determining a real man; but it varies from woman to woman depending again upon her expectations. It sometimes can be modified depending upon age and life experiences. This brings up a question I never fully answered in a prior chapter when I objected to my son's calling another man "daddy". The reason I didn't have an issue one way or the other with what my son decided was due to me being a real man about the situation. Prior to my son's birth, I was there for him and have been there for him throughout his entire life including after his mother's sudden passing in 1996. I know the struggles of single mothers throughout the country. There are a number of good men in this struggle along with me that never get the credit they so deserve because of all we hear concerning the negative stereotype of men. So a defining moment came in 2008 when a female friend gave me and four of my male friends gifts for no special occasion other than representing real men. As she explained, it was designed to acknowledge single parents, those who are working, striving and sacrificing for our kids, continuing to be positive role models, not only for our kids but setting standards for others in the neighborhoods as well. The gifts were nice but the thought and spirit of the gift will live long with us. The ironic part is that prior to my son's mother passing, we came to a mutual agreement, a signed contract, between us that covered every aspect of our son's welfare. This came about to a change within her household when she married and I felt certain things of her husband divorce decree and other support settlements greatly affected me as an active member of my son's life and welfare. I'm proud to say we both saw between our minor disagreements at that time and was able to mutually agree what was in the best interest of our son, sadly enough, after working out our differences in a written agreement- she passed unexpectedly six months later.

Below were some dating questions that originated during the course of the completion of my book. See if you can see yourself in any of the questions below.

1.Is having sexual relations on the first date a bad thing or mistake?
❑ Yes
❑ No

2.How long after dating a woman should a man expect or initiate sex? This coming from the theory after the third date the man expects sex.
❑ 1 week
❑ 2 to 3 weeks
❑ 1 month
❑ 1 to 3 months

3. This question is for men, does having a sexual relationship with a woman constitute a relationship?
❑ Yes
❑ No

4.Would you like to know or ask the number of one's prior sexual partners if you are considering a relationship/ committed relationship?
❑ Yes
❑ No

5.Would you date out of your race?
❑ Yes
❑ No

6.Would you date someone where there was at least a 15 years age difference?
❑ Yes
❑ No

7.Do you get upset when you see an attractive member of your race dating or in a relationship with someone of another race?
❑ Yes
❑ No

8.Do you think if women offered to buy a man a drink in a bar or night club it would be returned with gratitude and the man would in return buy her a drink in return?
❑ Yes
❑ No

9.Does a man or woman appear to me more attractive if they are with someone at the current time?
❑ Yes
❑ No

10.Would you make a choice of quantity rather than quality dating if you had to wait for your soul mate?
❑ Yes
❑ No

What Is a Real Man?

During the dialogue the question kept arising that I should get feedback from women in reference to their thoughts as to what a real man is. One actually gave her insight in a poem that she requested that I use.

Will The Real Man Please Stand UP!

What is a real man to me?

A God-fearing man who's not afraid
of following The Man Jesus

A man who marries a God-fearing woman
with a child takes them into his home, and
covers them with love.

Will the real man please stand up!

A man who gives a child his name and spoils her as if it was
his own. A man who loves his wife and submits himself unto
her as she submits herself to him.

A man who's not afraid of his wife accomplishments,
but yet encourages, supports and continually cherishes
and respect her.

A man who's not afraid of taking jobs to support his family.
A man who raises all of his children to respect and love everyone.
A man who believes if a family prays together the family
will stay together.

A man who looks after the elderly and takes the
responsibility upon himself that their needs are met.

Will the real man please stand up!

A man who encourages his children and tell them that they can do
all things through Christ who strengthens them.

Will the real man please stand up!

A man who shepherds his flocks, and tend to their
needs as though they were his own children.
A man who gives up his time unconditionally and
unselfishly to God's people.

Will the real man please stand up!

Thank you Courtney R. Johnson

Responses

• One who loves God, well rounded and responsible, good morals, values and one of his word. Trustworthy secure with himself, financially able to take care of his responsibility and provide for his family.

• Someone that is a provider, spiritual, selfless, humble, loving, compassionate, respectful, honest and don't have a problem in telling or showing his feelings. And don't have a problem in admitting that he is wrong sometime.

• A man who is knowledgeable, willing, ready and actively practicing the actions of providing, protecting, and proclaiming for the woman in his life with adequate sources while balancing his own needs and beliefs to make his life fulfilling.

• Real Man to me is a guy who respects me and treats me with gentleness and understanding, a man who I can rely on to the degree that I know that he will have my back in all situations.

• A real man would be someone that is honest, understanding, sensitive, a hard working provider all without complaints.

• A man who puts God first, who loves, protects, and provides for his woman, who's respectful to his woman and be the head of his family.

• A Real Man knows how to rule as head of his household to lead but can always take advice when needed. He does things necessary to make one happy even without asking, God fearing, loving, and caring with the love of family and has goals and achieves them. He is faithful, fun outgoing and knows how to lay it down.

• A real man is someone who is self-sufficient, confident, and has reached a point in his life that he is stable and has everything that is necessary to provide for his family.

• A real man is someone who handles his responsibilities, takes care of himself and seeks help or comfort when his direction is lost.

• A real man lives to be Christ like, he believes in Christ and knows how to communicate with Christ. A man who is patient, understanding and compromising but cautious. He's quite gentle yet firm. He's passionate, humorous, unpredictable and giving.

Quality Time

When I think of quality time in reference to dating and relationships a lot comes to mind but let's first explore the definition of the word <u>quality time</u>.

Quality time: is an informal reference to time spent with loved ones (e.g., close family, partners or friends) that is in some way important, special, productive or profitable. It is time that is set aside for paying full and undivided attention to the person or matter at hand. It may also refer to time spent performing some favorite activity.

Now we can proceed. I have spent countless hours in activities while dating and relationships, doing things that I really had no interest in. However, it was done with the intent that the activity would be reciprocated with an activity of my choosing at a later date and time. Let's just say I'm still waiting. If you are like me, you must fully agree that when dating, in the beginning, if you were lucky, several things came to mind like lunch dates, movies, theme parks, putt- putt golf, etc. However, when he or she thought you were in a relationship all ceased, so why is that? One should not get complacent in a relationship which can cause the other to feel taken for granted. The ironic part is that 75% of activities are inexpensive; they just require careful thought and a creative mind. I was speaking to a woman during the creation of this book who explained to me that her last relationship ended due to what he perceived as quality time which was him inviting her over so she could assist or complete his online class work for his degree. She explained afterwards that she would receive sex, which was good, and he would even hold her afterwards but this was the extent of quality time as he knew it.

Now as this relates to my agreement/ contract, I presented several singles with the concept while dating, the following guidelines are followed if they should present it to the person of interest in their life. Present the offer of each party coming up with two activities and during the course of a month on alternate weekends or depending on scheduling each would have to fully participate in each activity. This should cut down on the scrutiny of one always being presented with the notion that he or she only does what the other wants. It would also present the opportunity for one being exposed to new things and ideas and gives the chance to see each in a different light such as expense, planning, and one's true intent. The phrases, "you never take me out" and "we never do anything", and "we always do the same routine things" would cease. The main issue when one becomes complacent is it leads to several things with cheating included. If the dating makes it to the relationship stage, this will also be a good tool while dating to fully realize if the person is only out for self, is flexible, and, in turn, this practice could help you identify the character of the other person.

So at the end of the month, sit down and evaluate each other's regards to time spent, and it could be a determining factor on continuing the dating relationship. This way, the other can be introduced to the cost associated with dating if the person recommending the activity would be responsible for the cost for both parties. The "take me here, get tickets for this, and I want to go", would be clearly recognized by the other. At this stage, all expectations would be fully identified for the present and future and by participating in varying activities you will be seen in a different sense. This will address the definition of the word dating as it relates to fully defined quality time that's associated with it's value.

Also take the same theory in identifying how much time each has to offer the other. There's an old theory of dating of never accept a weekend date after Wednesday with the thought that he was not thinking of you in advance. When communicating, just ask how much time do you have for me? How often would you like to see me? This would free up any dating pressures. Remember, it's dating not a relationship. During the dating process many have sexual relations on occasion. This is also an area that could be addressed. Ask: What are your expectations of sexual activity on a daily, weekly or monthly basis? Also ask, if the individual would be sexually active with others since you are in the dating process? This would clear any and all thoughts of what he/ she is thinking, the stage or level of the relationship and it is therefore defined. This process will assist in setting the expectations of time, activity, and the ever important questions of sex.

Below are some additional questions that were identified during the dating process in reference to the subject matter.

1.Should a couple in a relationship also enter into a dating contract to keep the spark alive during the dating or courtship so one would not become content?
❑ Yes
❑ No

2.If he or she does not spend quality time with you after repeated talks involving the subject would you discontinue the relationship?
❑ Yes
❑ No

3.Should weekend getaways be agreed upon or enforced as it relates to quality time and possibly being a deal breaker in the relationship?
❑ Yes
❑ No

4.Should couples in dating and relationship phase have days set aside to see one another?
❑ Yes
❑ No

5.Have you ever dated a person and a Blockbuster night was his or her thought of quality time?
❑ Yes
❑ No

The Contract

Should Ones Expectations of Short and Long Term Goals Be Shared?

Let's begin by defining what a goal is: a desired result an animal, person or a system envisions, plans and commits to achieve—a personal or organizational desired end-point in some sort of assumed development. Many people endeavor to reach goals within a finite time by setting deadlines.

One of the many difficulties I experienced when re-entering the dating ranks were expectations of goals; whether short term or long term. When meeting individuals over the age of 30, many have already become parents, whether single parents or the result of prior marriages. With this, I would like to discuss the expectations of many that have yet to have married and some key factors facing someone you are dating or in a relationship with.

When I would meet a person of interest and after juggling her schedule pertaining to the kids, a continuing education was a key factor. Many women were continuing education in various fields of study which limited any remaining dating time. As it was explained to me, the new term the <u>independent woman</u> means she was not going to wait or depend on a man to provide for her welfare or the welfare of her children. Whether the field of study was for a short or long period of time one would have to support and respect such goals if you were to pursue any long standing committed relationship. I have witnessed both sides of the sexes support the opposite and stand- fast during trials of sacrifice only to have the relationship end as a result. When the goals were obtained in many cases the other decided to move in a different direction.

As a result, some discussion of a mutual contract should be adhered to in all fairness if one has fully supported along with the receiving party of the goal. Whether the goal is of education, business, a car or a house, one should understand that the sacrifices of two should not benefit just one. So once again, time invested in dating and relationships should be spelled out. When one party is finished with earning an advanced education and the financial benefit, should the other have any expectations of one's income, or share in the fruits of the other's labor without some sort of an agreement? Remember this is not a marriage partnership it is a relationship partnership. In the course of this book, I had the privilege of having dinner at a couple's home that a friend had invited me to. During the course of the evening a very attractive married couple in their mid- forties spoke of how they met and shared some of their beliefs of the dating issues of today. She explained that when her husband courted her that there was very little sexual activity prior to their marriage. She knew enough that she would be fully satisfied but that was not the main focus of their relationship but the growth potential of realizing that she had met her soul mate. At that time she made about 20K more than he and both made a sound investment in each other's future. During the time of courting, there was a shared belief, dream and agreement that one would make the necessary sacrifices for the family's future. Shortly after the marriage, the husband returned to college and obtained his Master's Degree that would further ensure security for the family in the future. Twelve years later, the husband now earns three times as that of his wife and both are happy and successful, each in their respected fields. So, in this case with a plan that was mutually agreed upon and executed to the fullest meant future success and prosperity and shared rewards.

1. Would you continue to date or enter into a relationship if someone did not fully support your goals and aspirations?
❑ Yes
❑ No

2. While dating someone or in a relationship has there ever been any type of jealousy or competition that changed the course of the stage of the relationship?
❑ Yes
❑ No

3. Would you enter into a relationship with someone that has no short term or long term goals and are complacent with the status quo?
❑ Yes
❑ No

4. Would you date or enter into a relationship if they have not achieved a high school diploma or will even try to obtain a GED?
❑ Yes
❑ No

5. If credit and income was no issue, would you enter into a relationship if one did not want to own a home?
❑ Yes
❑ No

6. Would you voice your opinion if you feel that the one you are in a relationship with is complacent with the aspects of one's life and you feel that he or she is cheating one's self?
❑ Yes
❑ No

7. Would you continue to date someone or enter into a relationship if all they desired to do was live pay check to paycheck?
❑ Yes
❑ No

8.Could you date or enter into a relationship with someone who was on public assistance, welfare, food stamps or Section Eight housing?
❑ Yes
❑ No

9.Would you date someone that was currently unemployed?
❑ Yes
❑ No

10.Would you date or enter into a relationship with someone who resided with family members but it was clear he/ she did not have their own place?
❑ Yes
❑ No

11.Would you object or say something to the person you were dating or in a relationship but not a committed relationship if they wanted to sleep over constantly either alone or with their kids due to their current living arrangements?
❑ Yes
❑ No

The Politics of Dating and Relationships

Politics: as a term is generally applied to the art or science of running governmental or state affairs, including behavior within civil governments but also applies to institutions, fields, and special interest groups such as the corporate, academic, and religious segments of society. It consists of "social relations involving authority or power" and to the methods and tactics used to formulate and apply policy.

Modern political discourse focuses on democracy and relationships. This pertains or relates to dating and relationships in that when no simple, clear agreements and/or contracts exists between individuals there is constant debating, guessing, and conflicts of issues that arise. Perhaps there is no clear resolution in mind or maybe a power play of one versus the other such as with Democrats versus Republicans.

One of the topics is <u>Dating Down</u> or when one refers to the fact that that person may or may not be on your level due to education, income, neighborhood, values, career, and other materialistic items.

To better define the subject I will lend this definition. *Dating down:- dating someone that is on a lower caliber as you or one who has not excelled as far as you have in any aspect.*

Where the dilemma comes into play is if you are truly seeking happiness and the one that you meet may have not excelled as far as you have in life. Is this an issue or a deal breaker? In years of the past people met, grew and would build together, but the issue with dating today is the lack of many of the foundational principles of relationships established long ago. We should revert back on dating principles or just ask our elders for advice concerning issues in our relationships due to certain events that have happened in a person's life causing some things to become unstable due to unemployment, injury, and divorce. This could resolve issues such as what friends and family may think about you bringing him or her home? Perhaps you look down on the person as a way to control this individual and it is you that fails to aspire to someone that you achieve their level or status. Remember, people come into your life for a reason and you can actually learn lessons from them all. Maybe you can inspire or motivate one at a point or maybe the opposite. The issue of dating down comes from one <u>settling</u> or thinking one can't do better. So this is where you ask yourself do I really want to pursue this person and keep them as a vital part of my life or can I do better? One should never say they are on a different level than the other because we are all one or two paychecks or a job loss away from joining whatever level you think they are on. Must we forget that it is all about being happy, two people coming together to share, laugh, and enjoy life?

So one should take the proper time to focus on one another to try and develop a friendship first, along with a mutual respect, prior to moving on to the next step. Attempt to at least focus on that person and put in the necessary time required and stop looking for the next best thing and learn the grass isn't always greener on the other side.

That brings me to the fact that other races meet, build together, sacrifice and do whatever is necessary to motivate and lift each other up. Sometimes we tear one another down from the very onset by not fully communicating and giving the proper time to grow. So how do we obtain the new aspiration of a Power Couple if we can't come to some sort of agreement between ourselves?

That brings several good questions as to where do singles meet? During the research for this project, I had the privilege of conversing with several waiters and waitresses and was able to obtain their take on dating. They revealed to me that there is a lot of games being played by both men and women and that they see serial daters daily and they can't see why and how the time, money and energy could be better focused as to maybe a hobby or part time job.

1.If you met someone that truly made you happy but later learned that their income, education level, and career or job was not that of yours, would you continue the dating process or relationship?

❑ Yes

❑ No

2.Is it an issue if you were dating or in a relationship with a woman and she made more money than you?

❑ Yes

❑ No

3.Could you continue to date someone if there credit was not to your standards?

❑ Yes

❑ No

4.Could you date or maintain a relationship with him or her if they lived with their parents?

❑ Yes

❑ No

5.Could you date or maintain a relationship with someone who did not have a car or was on some sort of public assistance?

❑ Yes

❑ No

6.Could you continue to date someone after learning that the person had been in jail or prison?

❑ Yes

❑ No

7.If you meet a lady in a fast food chain restaurant can you ask her on a date to the same or equal restaurant?

❑ Yes

❑ No

8.Is it appropriate to initiate contact with a woman when she is in the company of her children?

❑ Yes

❑ No

The Contract

Religion

Religion is a collection of cultural systems, beliefs systems and worldwide views that relate humanity to spirituality and, sometimes, to moral values. Many religions have narratives, symbols, traditions and sacred histories that are intended to rationalize life and the origin of life or the universe. They tend to derive morality, ethics, religious laws or a preferred lifestyle from their ideas about the cosmos and human nature.

I must admit when I met my now ex-wife, I was totally out of the church—a Christmas, Mother's Day and Easter (CME) attendee. This was far from the way I was raised as a Southern Baptist, where services I thought, lasted all day. When I became a teenager and was heavily into watching NFL football, church interfered with the Sunday's football action. We lived in an area of the country that was on Central Standard Time and the pastor was just beginning his sermon about the same time as football was starting. When you heard his opening words of "I'm not going to hold you long" that meant "OK, fourth quarter here I come." As this pertains to dating and relationships some have lost their way and may not attend church on a regular basis, if at all. So is this a major issue? What if the person knows and worships God in his or her own way and they have a personal relationship with God? Will you try to persuade your beliefs onto them? Or, will you attempt to negotiate a separate pattern or perspective? My belief was simple. As the man or head of my household, it was up to me to set the example for my son and stepson not to say one thing and do the other. However, this came with a little compromise. The church I joined after meeting my wife had two services, 7:30

a.m. and 9:30 a.m., and yes, you best believe I was in the early service when football season was in full effect! My mother and I had a similar agreement. I would attend services on the first and third Sundays of the month. I was required to attend on first Sunday due to the fact it was Communion Sunday. As strange as this may sound, but in both cases, a mutual agreement was ratified; however, some of the issues in today's dating and relationship pool are far greater.

I just wish the most troubling issues in dating relationships could be resolved in this mutual way. Should one insist on his or her mate attending church on a regular basis? In some cases even joining a church? This is the one major issue that came to the forefront when talking with several singles: the issue of religion and church. I thought the issue would be about if one was saved or even believed in God or maybe if there was a different religious practice. The results were all the same if the other would at least take an interest in church, this would not be such an issue or deal breaker. My oldest aunt was married to my uncle for 50 plus years until he passed in 2007. I actually verified this fact with my mother prior to typing this. The only two times I ever witnessed him in church was for the wedding of his two daughters. Actually, he had to be called back to the church during the last wedding because he left prior to the wedding photos being taken! This was quite ironic as my aunt, his wife, attended church every Sunday, went to Bible Study, choir rehearsal and served on what seemed like every board of the church since before I was born. Therefore, whatever understanding he had with my aunt worked just fine for them. So I guess they had a contract of some sorts?

1.If the person you were dating or in a relationship did not attend church on a regular basis, if at all, would you continue to interact with them?

❑ Yes
❑ No

2.If the person you were dating revealed to you that they were a non-believer in God would you continue in the dating or relationship?

❑ Yes
❑ No

3.If you are in a committed relationship should you attend the same church and services together?

❑ Yes
❑ No

The Contract

Timing

*Timing: is the control of time and speed of action
or event so it occurs at the proper moment.*

There is nothing like that old phrase, it's all about timing, but in business it's all about location, location, location. You must continue the dating process until you meet that special someone and hopefully you will be able to identify him/ her. Some of the dating excuses I've identified are as follows: a person just has no time to date because of work, school and kids. The person may have just ended a relationship and/ or marriage and need time to heal. In addition, they could be in their man or woman hating stages or in the "I'm just going to do me" time period of their life. Some are in the midst of possibly moving but the most popular one I've experienced is everyone I'm interested in is already taken. If it is any comfort, time is supposedly on your side and patience is a virtue.

People go through timing stages for various reasons. Sometimes with men, its either feast or famine, meaning there are plenty of women at various times and when you are in a drought there are none to be found. One thing with timing is the temptation it causes when your dating life picks up. As you deal with timing; be cool, calm and collected this time to will pass. During a recent 4th of July cookout I was attending, I put to the test some of these theories. I had the pleasure of meeting a married couple of 54 years. I was explaining some of the dating issues and the lady stated that in her opinion this generation doesn't know the meaning of the word <u>Love</u> and it is easily confused with the word <u>lust</u>. She explained that individuals don't truly communicate but see the physical and don't take time to get to know one another; therefore, they are wasting their time in the long run on both ends. I expressed this to my best friend, his lady and one other couple in the room that when it comes to a relationship I have two simple rules. Prior to stating the rules, I gave the following disclaimer which was please don't read into the rules and let me state both rules: number one: don't read into the question and number two: this logic has kept marriages together forever. Again, I repeated the disclaimer and stated forever! The rules were as follows: "rule number one: do what I say, when I say, how I say, and don't ask any questions." "rule number two: when in doubt, see rule number one." Let's just say the looks I received from the individuals in the room were as if I was a crazed lunatic! However, as I continued with a little latitude, I asked one question of a popular television series in the 1970's, Good Times, and asked who was the head, or ran the family? All in the room stated the male character, James, the father; I objected and said, "No". It was the mother's character, "Florida". As I fully explained my logic, my advice to them was to think back to all the episodes and acknowledge that James was the head of the family and perceived to be in charge cause he was the male. However, all of the decisions made for the household were run through Florida with a simple process of communicating one's issues and thoughts, in private and not in front of the family. Florida was the rational one and James, being the head, deferred to Florida's decisions as long as Florida didn't disrespect him in front of the family and friends. This is a lost art: Allowing the man to think he's in charge but the woman is actually running the family. I received a high five from the older woman while her husband sat in silence and smiled.

Another aspect that needs to be considered is if each individual is whole. If not, one can't fully give themselves to the other. How could one fully behold and expect one enter into your life to complete you, if you are a work in progress yourself? It was explained to me that her husband courted her from the very beginning and it was her time because she was whole and was able to receive at that time what he had to offer. People replace love with lust when they are not complete because they don't really know what they are truly looking for and their judgment is clouded. They want others to provide from day one, with the exception of ideas and material things that they can't provide for themselves. As I dwelled on this for a minute it made me think of a commercial that runs in the Atlanta area about a trade school. A man and woman are standing at the bus stop waiting for a bus, the man asked the woman out on a date and she replied, "What are we going to do? Ride the bus together?" The man stated " I got to get it together." Later in the commercial the same woman is at the bus stop, the same man pulls up in a fancy sports car and speaks to her, "Can I get your number?" Then she gets into his car. My thinking is a little different in this aspect. I think he should wait for her to get her life together, but that's just me. So as it relates to timing, what if we have already met our one true soul mate and didn't realize it due to certain circumstances in life. Are we promised a replacement of sort? As I can attest, like most men, we run pass a few that we truly think could be the one. I look forward to living life without any regrets by pondering on what could have been if only I had done this or that or by trying to get someone back.

Another rule of thought when it comes to timing comes from the hit song by Beyonce... ("You Should Have Put a Ring On It.") Where a man should have stepped up to the plate in the past and placed a ring on the finger of his then woman, some would say he is a <u>real man</u>. In any event, I try to realize that all things in life happen for a reason. So the key is the ability to be open no matter what the circumstances in one's life, the determination to let go of some old baggage, and ending relationships that are not healthy. How can one receive your blessing and aspire to identify as your soul mate if you are clinging to something that is not good for you? We all possess the where withal to enter into a relationship but we don't know how to end a relationship. I've been known to give some good advice to both male and females on occasion; however, when it came to taking my own advice, it was very difficult because I was emotionally involved in the situation and couldn't realize that maybe due to my arrogance, that I was destined to fail in all attempts to reconcile the relationship. At best, I was putting a bandage on the situation and in due time it would all surface and come to fruition. So as timing is essential, one must determine when to move along. A perfect example is the things that both sexes do to block or keep someone else from advancing to date or proceed into a relationship. It's like a monkey bar effect when one fully knows the value he or she currently has and will test the waters in secret to determine if anything is better. If they can't find a suitable prospect they swing back to you and proceed with the relationship. This is a major issue that many encounter with dating, when one is honestly trying to pursue a person but is unaware that the other person is currently in love, in a relationship, or on hiatus with someone else. This is what I refer to as dating you've warmed her up, <u>catered</u> and <u>sponsored</u> her for the evening, only to have the date end with the ex or love interest, coming over to the person's house and this individual seals the deal with a late hour <u>booty call</u>. Until this individual can identify the source of those actions and discontinue this behavior, you will forever be the nice guy.

1.Should one accept dates or ask someone out on a date if he/ she is not over the prior relationship?
❑ Yes
❑ No

2.If you are truly not interested in someone would you tell them that they are wasting their time prior to the date?
❑ Yes
❑ No

3.Have you ever had sex with someone that you were not into just to get the last person off your mind?
❑ Yes
❑ No

4.Should you date people that reside within your subdivision, apartment complex or work environment?
❑ Yes
❑ No

5.Since women and men communicate differently should one fully spell out ones true intent to define what type of relationship they are seeking and willing to provide?

❏ Yes

❏ No

6.Should you continue to go on dates with him/ her if you are not feeling that person even though you have a good time and he or she expectations are different from yours?

❏ Yes

❏ No

7. Is it possible to love two different people at the same time?

❏ Yes

❏ No

8. Is it possible to have sex over a period of time with someone with no strings attached and not develop feelings?

❏ Yes

❏No

The Contract

Horoscope Signs

Horoscope: The aspect of the planets and stars at a given moment, such as the moment of a person's birth, used by astrologers.

A diagram of the signs of the zodiac based on such an aspect. An astrological forecast, as of a person's future, is based on a diagram of the aspect of the planets and stars at a given moment. Astrological readings examine the powerful alignments of the sun, moon, planets, and stars at the time of your birth. Those alignments, as well as the continual movements of the heavens throughout your life, have a strong influence on your personality, success, and the relationships you create. Analysis of your astrological signs and current astrological conditions can provide essential insight on your past, your present, and your future. It can also predict how you will get along with others, based on their astrological charts.

I must first admit I'm a Taurus and as far as Zodiac signs are concerned, I've discovered that some won't date me or others due to our zodiac sign. As I examine the above definition and with all due respect, you're telling me my true happiness is caused by the alignment of the moon, stars, and planets? Well I know I'm on planet earth and man has landed on the moon and the sun is hot- now can I get your number? My thought is my personality will be the same if I was born in the prior or later month. It's society and my upbringing that has made me who and what I am. Now again, how I can I learn more about you? So understanding your horoscopes and that of your mate or future mate will inform you on how we will get along in the future? Let's just say I will treat you like a lady and I'm a gentleman. How can you learn that if I'm not given the chance to show such? I in turn ask myself, is this one of the reasons why I'm single?

1.Do you believe in the theory of compatibility of zodiac signs when dating and pursuing relationships?
❑ Yes
❑ No

2.Would you date or enter into a relationship with someone whose zodiac sign stated that you were incompatible?
❑ Yes
❑ No

Technology and Dating

I must admit in the technology area I'm somewhat behind the times and trying to catch up. I have been described by some in the past as a caveman in some areas; meaning if I meet a woman I should just hit her over the head with my club and pull her back to my cave. This is best described as 20th century old school meets 21st century values. In all honesty technology is good and some areas it is bad while taking into the account the internet craze of on-line dating. On the plus side, it gives you a chance to meet individuals you would not ordinarily meet in daily life. However, it also connects you with a plentiful amount of individuals as well and if there is no meeting of the minds/ agreement the same process that brought you together will soon set you apart.

I've been in several restaurants in past years and could immediately identify individuals who were on their first date or appeared to have been meeting for the first time. The focus was on each other and not their IPads and cell phones, constantly checking text, emails, or receiving calls. In the same restaurant you can easily identify couples that were not on first dates by the continued use of electronic devices. Their attention was elsewhere and not on each other. So sometimes it is easier to text or email someone but the old school theory still exists that a nice phone call would better serve the purpose. Sometimes texts messages and emails can and will be taken out of context depending upon the persons mood when receiving it. Sadly, the same piece of technology can also be used to end relationships. A coward's way to break up would be through text message or email instead of giving a common <u>courtesy</u> call or meeting in person. Sometimes the same avenue of technology that brought you together and communicated at convenient times can also be served as a downfall in the end when technology can be used as a tool for cheating. You can be in each other's presence while your significant other is texting or emailing to arrange future contact or a rendezvous with someone else. Just as a reminder; with the advancement in technology it increases the chances of getting busted. With everyone having camera phones and social media status alerts, you don't have a chance these days. So welcome to dating and relationships 21st Century style. I only ask what will the future bring?

1.On a first date should one refrain from the use of cell phones, IPads, or other electronic devices that takes away from the attention of the date?
❑ Yes
❑ No

2.Would you make a comment in a respectful way to your date if he/she continued the use of an electronic device that was proven not to be an emergency situation?
❑ Yes
❑ No

3.While in a relationship or committed relationship is it appropriate to answer each other's phone?
❑ Yes
❑ No

4.While in a relationship or committed relationship should one have access to the others pass codes to phone and emails accounts?
❑ Yes
❑ No

5.Do you think the use of technology has helped or hindered the dating/ relationship process?
❑ Yes
❑ No

6.Would you subscribe to a dating website?
❑ Yes
❑ No

7.Have you or would you ever consider the use of any type of electronic device to monitor the person you were in a relationship with?
❑ Yes
❑ No

8. If you thought your mate was cheating and somehow you gained access to their cell phone, email, facebook, financial accounts, or diary would you use it to your benefit?
❑ Yes
❑ No

The Contract

Top 5 Deal Breakers of Internet Dating

- Misrepresentation of oneself in one's photo
- Location or geographically unavailable
- Serial Dater
- Bad Hygiene
- Talks to much about sex

The Contract

Temptation or Cheating

Temptation: is the desire to perform an action that one may enjoy immediately or in the short term but will probably later regret for various reasons: legal, social, psychological (including feeling guilt, health-related, economic, etc. In the context of religious temptation, it is the inclination to sin. Temptation also describes the coaxing or inducing a person into committing such an act, by manipulation or otherwise of curiosity, desire or fear of loss.

Cheating: refers to an immoral way of achieving a goal. It is generally used for the breaking of rules to gain advantage in a competitive situation. The rules infringed may be explicit, or they may be from an unwritten code of conduct based on morality, ethics or custom, making the identification of cheating a subjective process. Cheating can refer specifically to marital infidelity.

When I think of these two words together as it aligns with my thought process, one would first need to have an agreement and/ or contract so one wouldn't feel tempted to cheat. In relationships and committed relationships it is best to have some type of understanding so both individuals are on the same page so if one is tempted or tested, it won't be referred to as cheating. One wouldn't feel that he/ she has cheated if there wasn't ever any temptation. The logic is simple, what one may refer to as cheating may not be cheating in the mind of another. Some say cheating is sexual intercourse with a person other than the one in which you are in a relationship/committed relationship. Some may say the mere thought of the temptation alone is cheating. The logic would be, could you go home and tell him or her verbatim what you have done? Yes, that would be the gray area. Some say, in the earlier example that going out with the person on a date without your mate's knowledge is cheating. So once again, if the issue of boundaries is discussed and guidelines are established for a future pattern of behavior, this should be put to rest.

If I wanted to discuss the reason men cheat it would vary from man to man, the same could be said for women. So when I hear the reason someone cheated on me and the other person says that they were not in a relationship, some obvious signs were missed along the way. For example: let's say a couple is dating or seeing one another on a consistent basis, and a key is given to the woman to the man's home for convenience purposes because of the man's late night work schedule, so that they may see each other at a late hour. Later in the dating period, it was revealed that the man had sexual relations with a "friend." Was this cheating? The man was under the impression that they were dating cause a week earlier a moment came and passed where a song was playing on the radio where the lyrics stated "we don't go together we just kicking it". So in the man's thought process, they were not in a relationship. This is the state of most dating relationships. There is no discussion surrounding the issue that evolves into a mutual understanding or agreement identifying the nature of the relationship and the exact identification of the current status. The lesson learned from this was that some would say he was cheating. Some could say otherwise. Nevertheless, the lesson learned is that some take it that if you have a key to their home, they're spending the night daily, and having sexual relations on a regular basis that this constitutes a relationship. This was not a hypothetical situation but one that hits very close to home. The man learned a valuable lesson and was never fully able to make amends. Not of the act itself but the failed communication that was taken for granted and the mistaken signs that were given to the woman. So in this case, does the temptation followed by the act of cheating make the man a cheater? In this situation, all she wanted was the truth and the reason for the cheating. The truth will hurt only once but a lie will kill and end a relationship. So I decided to be open to all questions she raised. In this case, the same respect that I was given from her much the same was required in return.

Other lessons I have learned in the singles arena following my divorce was the nature of disrespect for individuals currently married or in relationships. In this reference, I will only discuss relationships. The old school notion of one being off the market or taken is not respected these days. Such as, if I did meet someone and was in the early stages, men would try their best to interrupt the relationship, sometimes with you being nearby. I wouldn't call this temptation but disrespect and avoid speaking on this issue would be a disservice. If a man or woman indicates that they are in a relationship why continue to press the issue? I observed a scenario in which a person tried to talk to a lady friend of mine. He pressed the issue by saying "Statistics show that most relationships last only 4 to 5 months, so why not have my number handy?" It is good to flirt but downright ignorant to pursue where you are not wanted. Some take your kindness for a weakness in this area. A female friend told me how she busted her man cheating by way of a magazine. She explained what brought it to her attention from the onset was his suspicious behavior but there was nothing she could prove at the time. So as he departed from her home, he left a magazine with the subscription mailing address of another woman on the cover. Being the woman that she is, she quickly performed a records search of the name and address and identified a home number and contacted the owner of the magazine and realized that she was not alone in the relationship. So upon his return to her home later in the evening, he was confronted with the facts not only from her but also his other woman as well. The lesson is if you are going to cheat you will eventually get caught!

1.During the dating process, does having sexual relations with each other constitute a relationship?
❏ Yes
❏ No

2.Have you ever been in a relationship where your mate cheated on you?
❏ Yes
❏ No

3.Have you ever cheated on the person you were involved in a relationship or committed relationship with?
❏ Yes
❏ No

4.Is there a double standard, meaning men are hypocrites, when it comes to cheating?
❏ Yes
❏ No

5.If a woman stated that she was celibate or practiced the 90 -day rule would you continue dating her or continue in the relationship?
❏ Yes
❏ No

6.If you saw your best friend's man or woman out on a date with another person of the opposite sex would you tell your best friend?
❑ Yes
❑ No

7.Could you continue in the relationship or committed relationship after he/she has cheated on you?
❑ Yes
❑ No

8.Is knowing the graphic and intimate details of the cheating good for closure or healing process?
❑ Yes
❑ No

9.Would there be less cheating and less confusion if members of each sex, held one's counterparts responsible for the actions of their gender?
❑ Yes
❑ No

10.Is the term once a cheater always a cheater accurate?
❑ Yes
❑ No

11. Does having a key to the residence of the person you are dating mean that you are in a relationship?
❑ Yes
❑ No

A Defined Approach on Dating/ Relationships

The Contract

A Discussion on One's Sexual History

There are certain events that take place in your life where you can remember where you were and what you were doing at a particular date and time. Mine was in November 1991, I was in the State Patrol Academy when I was watching basketball superstar Earvin "Magic" Johnson announced he had tested positive for the HIV virus. Looking back at that time period in my life, I must honestly admit that I, like most, didn't practice safe sex on each and every occasion. I was single and fresh out of the military, this was a true wake up call for me. If "Magic" is not immune, then neither am I. Like millions of Americans, this was my wake up call to use condoms on each sexual encounter from that point forward. Looking back at my sexual history then, and how it has changed until the present, I am very blessed to have tested negative for HIV/AIDS. The question is, at what stage of the dating relationship should one trust the other enough to engage in unprotected sex? Should both parties' have a physical to show documentation of their respective medical history? How much should one reveal about previous sexual history? Should they reveal the number of prior partners? If there were any same sex partners or if one is either bi-sexual or homosexual? Not until I moved to Atlanta in 1992 was I asked the question, was I gay, bi or ever been with a man. At first I was offended, but then learned that this was a standard question now in the singles and dating relationship arena. As I would find out many years later I would also be asking the same questions to women that I was pursuing. Are you married? Do you have a boyfriend or a girlfriend? You would be surprised at the number of times that I have had to ask that question. The only dumb question is the one not asked or explored.

I can't tell you the number of women I have come in contact with that are bisexual? The answers varied and in some way, shape, form or fashion whether there was some type of experimentation in the past, whether it is was a <u>swinger's</u> lifestyle or some type of threesome. So what are you to do upon receiving this information? Do you continue and be somewhat judgmental? In many instances, men are hypocrites in this area. What type of discussion or agreement should be the focus? Maybe testing and any type of birth control one may practice? A similar agreement should be brought to the forefront as it relates to any sexual tapes that may or may not surface in the future during the course of the relationship. These are instant deal breakers as well as any involvement in swinger's clubs or lifestyle. The focus is that you are entrusting or investing your time, energy, and life in the hands of another. How many prior sexual partners are too many? Opinions will vary upon age, lifestyle, gender, etc. Women say this is a touchy issue for men so some always give a fictitious number when asked. So should one ask? What is too many sexual partners for a man or woman? A single person dating and actively pursuing a relationship from the adult age of 18 to say 50 has sex with two people (separate) per month since the age of 18 to the age of 50. At this rate that would be at a ratio of 24 individuals per year for 32 years with the grand tally of 768 sexual partners. Take this standard and say if this was a man what title would be given? Would the title be different if it were a woman? If so, why?

On this footnote, reverse the tales a little and calculate if a woman had a prior sexual relationship of the same sex would she be considered a lesbian? If a man had a prior sexual relationship with a man would he be viewed as bi-sexual or gay? The hypocritical views of these questions are very puzzling and people have different viewpoints. The main focus should be whether or not this is a deal breaker in dating and relationships? For years, men were thought to have women into three categories: the marrying type, the ones for sex only that you never take out in public, and the in the meantime category that you have no intention on marrying. They are just for having a good time. So with knowing one's past, would this change your viewpoint of the person you are in a relationship with or possibly end the dating aspect? Take this viewpoint to another level. Could you date or enter into a relationship with someone but later gain knowledge that the person had been sexually active with one of your closest friends? So either knowing or not having the knowledge of this is a key factor. A mutual understanding or defined look at the viewpoints of another should be fully explored? After returning from the Essence Music Festival in 2012, a female friend shared a story she was privy to while in the ladies' bathroom. While talking with her friends in the bathroom, a nice, attractive lady who was under the influence shared some knowledge with them and stated that "she is the Dick Destroyer"; referencing her exposure to the HIV virus she had obtained from a man. Her sole purpose was to sleep with as many men possible during the course of the weekend and expose them to the virus as well. It was explained to me that she was very serious. These thoughts were expelled while a little under the influence, but I could see that every word she said she meant. I wasn't present for the festival but have heard of strange sexual liaisons of grown men and women like it was Freaknick in the mid 1990's in Atlanta.

1. If you learned while dating or in a relationship that your mate had a high number of prior sexual partners would you end the relationship?
❑ Yes
❑ No

2. If while dating or pursuing a relationship it was revealed that your mate did not practice safe sex would you discontinue the relationship?
❑ Yes
❑ No

3. During the dating process, should you divulge that you have had multiple sexual partners?
❑ Yes
❑ No

4.If he/she revealed that they were celibate or practice the 90-day rule would you continue to date them or pursue the relationship?
❏ Yes
❏ No

5. Could you name all of your prior sexual partners by name?
❏ Yes
❏ No

6. If the person you were dating or in a relationship with revealed he/she had an STD in this case herpes would you continue in the relationship?
❏ Yes
❏ No

7.How long after dating a woman or in a relationship should a man expect sex?
❏ 1 week
❏ 2 to 3 weeks
❏ One month
❏ 1 to 3 months

8.Would you ask the person you were dating about the number of prior sexual partners?
❏ Yes
❏ No

9.If your partner revealed that he/ she had sexual relations with a partner of the same sex would you discontinue the relationship?
❏ Yes
❏ No

10.If a woman had sexual relations with a woman would she be considered a lesbian?
❏ Yes
❏ No

11. If a man revealed he had sexual relations with a same sex partner would he be considered gay?
❏ Yes
❏ No

12. Would you insist on a physical prior to having unprotected sex with someone you were dating or in a relationship with?
❏ Yes
❏ No

13. While dating or in a relationship you found out that he/she had been sexually active with one of your closest friends would you discontinue the dating/ relationship?
❏ Yes
❏ No

14. Is there a grace or time period when dating an ex of a friend?
❏ Yes
❏ No

15. If the person you were involved in a relationship with ask you to join in a threesome what would your answer be?
❏ Yes
❏ No

16. If the person you were in a relationship with refused to take a physical to advance the relationship would you discontinue the relationship?
❏ Yes
❏ No

The Contract

An Agreement on Holiday, Birthday and Anniversary Gifts

There is an unwritten rule with men that during the summer months we elect to find some reason to maneuver away from relationships for whatever reason during the Christmas season to Valentine's Day, we have some type of issues with ourselves that we must seek a solution that does not involve you.

As this pertains to gift giving for holidays, birthdays, in the dating and relationship stage I tend to be very curious as to why we do such things? These are the beginning stages of relationships and most may elect not to give gifts to ease any confusion; however, some believe that the gift defines the state or level of the relationship. So when should we be expected to provide a gift during the dating stages if there is no commitment? Some may say that if sexual relations are involved, you should give a gift. That is a question that everyone will have different opinions on. I ask why not have a discussion of an agreement if there will be a gift exchange and maybe ask a cost expectation range. The reason for this discussion is that even though this is a communication breakdown that has happened long before the gift or holiday it can be rectified but again the problem is also with the unclear expectations of the other.

A female I was conversing with told me after dating her current boyfriend for a year, but living in separate houses, she went all out for his birthday. In the past he had indicated that he had never had a birthday party and she, being a giver, went the whole nine for him. This was her nature; however, less than two weeks later it was her birthday and she received only a card. So in this case what was the real issue? How were their signals mixed? Why were expectations not met to satisfy both? The lesson that was learned in the situation is never to lose yourself while trying to possibly hold on to a relationship or someone who demonstrates that they don't care about losing you. Was one giving with the expectation of getting a better gift in return or was it just that person nature and them expressing themselves? Was this a defining moment in the relationship and many relationships like this one ended shortly thereafter?

Should there be an agreement on gift giving? In many instances one of the persons could have a completely differently outlook from the one that is into the holiday or birthday. This is another form of stress that comes with dating and relationships that could be avoided with some type of mutual agreement. Yes, it may sound strange but long after this subject has been discussed it will continue to haunt dating and relationships. Let's not even speak of the pressures of Valentine's Day, as men sometimes don't fully communicate what women are to them, just remember the definition of the word dating. This single day could cause men to go broke with a woman's expectations of him.

1.During what stage of a dating relationship should one expect to receive a gift for birthday, Valentine's Day or Christmas?
❑ Yes
❑ No

2.Should there be a price discussion or agreement on the exchange of gifts?
❑ Yes
❑ No

3.Should gifts ever be returned if the relationship ended a short period of time after it was given?
❑ Yes
❑ No

4. If you are in the early dating stage is a man required to purchase gifts for Valentine's Day?
❑ Yes
❑ No

5. Should more than one gift be given when his/her birthday falls on Christmas, Valentine's Day or an anniversary?
❑ Yes
❑ No

The Contract

Income

Income: is the consumption and savings opportunity gained by an entity within a specified time frame that is generally expressed in monetary terms. However, for households and individuals, "income is the sum of all the wages, salaries, profits, interests payments, rents and other forms of earnings received... in a given period of time.

There is no romance without finance. So the issue of finances when meeting one another is a major part of the dating and relationship arena. The day of two coming together as one and building together is a thing of the past. Therefore, the concern here is if the money of the potential mate a major deal breaker? It is true that no one wants to struggle; however, the times most joyous in my life came when there was a struggle and the times when I was happy with the financial aspect of my life, there was no one there to share it with. My goal now is to find a happy medium. No, I don't want to struggle but why does one's income level factor into the equation? If the person truly makes you happy but they are not at the income level you are would that cause you not to continue with the relationship? Remember, there is someone that may look down on you in this same scenario. A person's income is different from that of <u>dating down or settling</u>. It's an imaginary line of where should the person entering your life is. A few things should be factored into this equation: job loss, child support, and the current economy. Again, people enter your life for a reason and it is up to you to identify and learn of the advantages and disadvantages of the lessons. Instead of judging one's income maybe you actually improve it if the individual is willing. A reminder, just because a person is at a lower income than you does not mean that the person may not be whole, content, or happy with where they are in their life. Their lifestyle may be adjusting to you so maybe you may have to adjust yours to their level.

Some individuals raised issues, if a woman earned more than the man? Would there be additional challenges and who is the head of the household and difficulties in the respect level? A job or income does not define a man's character. So when I speak of income, I just say as long as your expectations of another does not exceed thoughts you have for yourself or a <u>come up</u>. A research study showed that the number of black women who are college graduates far exceeded that of black males. With this trend will the future heads of households be women due to the higher education and higher income levels? As this relates to the dating and relationship phase, what is a man's future role? Has it been modified and the expectations defined differently? In lieu of this trend, do we get a pass on buying drinks in bars and night clubs? Will this raise an issue in any disagreements in the household and this fact be pointed out in that circumstance? As this pertains to me, I have dated women in the past whose income exceeded mine, but the most important thing is it's not how much you make but can one provide and take care of one's business for the household. I would say the term " real man " does apply in holding ones on. So it's not how much you make its how much you can save or keep for yourself.

In a recent discussion with a female friend, she stressed the importance of a man's income and his ability to sustain a family and her lifestyle. I asked if there was a certain income level that she required to meet her expectations. I gave her a scenario of a man making about 24K per year and if he was able to save 25% of his income and another 25 % went to bills she stated that wasn't enough, and she <u>wanted</u> more. Using this example, how do we meet the expectations of others? I tried another example, if she were to move in with the man in his modest 3 bedroom home along with her two children and he ask for nothing in living expenses. The trade -off would be she would save on her prior living expenses that was about 16K per year.

In this example she replied yes due to what she made she kept and the man fully provided but in this instance he secured all of her <u>needs</u> and she was able to provide her wants. The irony in this example was that it was the same man in both cases, so we shouldn't be quick to judge another. We should mutually identify one's strength and work with it rather than the weakness of the perceived lack of income. In today's relationship arena, the expectation of man meets the harsh reality. This same female friend had previously identified that in a prior relationship that her man suffered from job loss and the difficulties in the failure of him starting his own business. She also expressed that any one she met should have a substantial income. As I have learned with substantial incomes comes the perception that those individuals are doing well. So I decided to test myself and sent out 5 emails to five female friends on a study of myself and requested that each judge me on what they know of me and where I rank with others in my age group in reference to the so called important things in life, income, house, car, and education. I asked that they grade me on a scale of 1 to 10. I was trying to determine how someone sees me out of a fresh pair of eyes and the perception of how we rank material things in life as success and if I had made it yet. I've heard in the past that a man at age 30 should have achieved this or at age 40 should be stable and at this level. In this theory no one takes in account life's trials and tribulations that when you meet someone you don't know their struggle.

So I ask this question; when a couple divorce why is it easier for a woman to move on and expect the man entering her life to have his life together but if that same man exiting from that relationship has to start fresh and feel a sense of remorse to anyone entering his life? Is this due to one seeking for another to complete them and make them whole? So does income define one as a person? The old saying the more you make will be the more you spend and in this economy many have been a casualty to job loss, foreclosure, and bankruptcy. So the man making 24k could have just recently filed bankruptcy and now has a solid grip on his finances due to a restructuring plan while many may be making six figures will be heavy in debt. The myth with this as it relates to dating is that I hear both sides state that they don't want anyone with bad credit. I ask you who among us after the Bush Era are whole and unscathed? The irony is the person that usually expects or requires a certain credit score thinking is somewhat like a foreclosure or bankruptcy in that you're putting the value of your expectations on the other person and maybe in your prior relationship you invested way too much and should have ended the relationship long ago. Because what you put in far outweighed the value of the relationship. So one should just cut their losses and restructure just what a bankruptcy does. One should have a fresh start and become whole again prior to meeting the next person that enters into your life. The myth is you're a failure and will lose all and that credit is the key. Many of us have been ignorant to certain laws that other races have used to their success and benefit. Now to answer the question of my grade from the self- assessment I received from others, the average score was a 7.5.

The reason for this was for me to fully identify individuals entering my life to use a measuring stick to use as a tool in the evaluation for any expectations of their needs. I try to use this as a tool in dating and relationships to identify any and all attraction to individuals meaning why am I dating her? Is it for the physical attraction which far outweighs the substance of what I was truly seeking? If you choose to go with the physical and the physical only, I learned life's, lesson all too well that your debt ratio will soon increase and some of the above options may be sought, but prior to that aspect I was able to identify the pressures of all wanting that knockout 10. All things that look good may not truly be good for me. It was pointed out to me years ago and I still try to practice this today. I once was in a relationship that caused me much headache just due to looks and physical attraction and the woman being the envy of all men. Luckily after 2 plus years I was able to identify this and as Clint Eastwood said "a man has got to know his limitations". Should one be defined by money? The days of people meeting and having acceptance to each other at that current stage in one's life is a thing of the past. If there is no defined agreement in this area the answer to why pursue a relationship is truly lost.

1. Would the man still be considered the head of the household if he was not the primary bread winner?
❏ Yes
❏ No

2.If a woman asks a man out on a date should she pay?
❏ Yes
❏ No

3.Would you date someone on public assistance, living in section 8 housing or receiving food stamps?
❏ Yes
❏ No

4.If living together should the woman pay more expenses since she made a higher salary?
❏ Yes
❏ No

5.Would you date or enter into a relationship with a woman if she made considerable more money than you?
❏ Yes
❏ No

6. If the person you were dating revealed that he/ she had credit issues as it related to bankruptcy or foreclosure would you continue to date them?
❏ Yes
❏ No

7.Is the saying true that women marry for money first then love the second time?
❏ Yes
❏ No

8.Should one reveal early in the dating stage of one's past credit issues, foreclosure or bankruptcy?
❏ Yes
❏ No

The Contract
120

A Defined Discussion of Loans or Gifts

Loan: is a type of debt. Like all debt instruments, a loan entails the redistribution of financial assets over time, between the lender and the borrower. The loan is generally provided at a cost, referred to as interest on the debt, which provides an incentive for the lender to engage in the loan. In a legal loan, each of these obligations and restrictions is enforced by contract, which can also place the borrower under additional restrictions known as covenants.

Gift: or a present is the transfer of something without the expectation of payment. Although gift-giving might involve an expectation of reciprocity, a gift is meant to be free. In many human societies, the act of mutually exchanging money, goods etc. may contribute to social cohesion. Economists have elaborated the economics of gift-giving into the notion of a gift economy. By extension the term gift can refer to anything that makes the other happier or less sad, especially as a favor, including forgiveness and kindness.

One piece of advice I learned from my father is, if you loan someone some money and they don't give it back, what can you do? So a good rule of thumb is don't loan any more than you can afford to lose. As it relates to dating and relationships, there's a wide range of expectations, assumptions, and sometimes demands. Living in the metro Atlanta area, I've asked the age old question, is it my responsibility to pay certain bills for women? Lights, gas, and rent? Better yet, is it my responsibility to pay for the upkeep of hair, nails, etc.? This is one of the major issues of dating and relationships. What constitutes or in what time frame is one required to assist in the responsibilities of another? This is a major concern for men that I have found and I can most certainly relate to. The expression you have to pay the cost to be the boss is nice; however, in the age of the so called <u>independent woman</u> enough is enough. In today's economy, two is better than one but actually the words are can I borrow or can I get is often asked in the dating stage. So don't start something that you can't see through until the end. Does having sexual relations with a woman make one responsible for certain bills or is this simply another form of prostitution? I know that's a bit extreme but think about it. At what stage is a man required, if any, to take on such responsibility?

In numerous situations while dealing with women in the past, there was a clear understanding that any exchange of funds was a clear loan. It was stated that way when it was given and when it was requested. I'm just saying that after the money has exchanged hands; don't hold your breath on getting it back. Not all cases end this way but the majority do! Just ask any <u>real man</u>. It wouldn't be so hard but in today's time women have no idea how hard it is to be a man: the demands, expectations, and pressures of society… but then add in dating, yes dating not a committed relationship for the exchange of funds. I ask if there should be a clear and precise mutual agreement in this area? After all, money is business. Just think of this in the dating stage. Should a man have available funds for each that he is dating? Remember as in any friendship, a quick way to lose a friend is over money when there is no clear agreement with the expectation concerning its return.

As I watch some daytime reality court shows, I've come to learn the number one defense in these cases, in the mind of the defendant, was the plaintiff stated it was a <u>gift</u> when providing the funds. So in the receiver's or defendant's mind, when they asked the question of money they clearly said can you gift or give me some money, meaning don't expect it back. Understand this scenario goes both ways and what I have seen or witnessed is sorry ass men living off women. It is sad "I have never received or even asked a woman for a dime." This subject is far different from when men are expected to purchase drinks in clubs for women or even with the cost of gas? It has been brought to my attention that women now ask for some type of gas allowances in certain circumstances. So when it comes to the subject of money, it is a very touchy indeed. And somehow, sex and money somehow go hand in hand. So was sex expected as repayment or was money expected due to the relationship?

1.Is it appropriate to loan money to someone that you are dating?
❑ Yes
❑ No

2.Have you ever loaned money to someone that you were in a relationship with and never had the money returned?
❑ Yes
❑ No

3.If you were to loan money to someone you were dating or in a relationship with, would you insist on a written agreement?
❑ Yes
❑ No

4.Should a man ever ask for a loan from a woman he was dating or in a relationship with?
❑ Yes
❑ No

5.Depending on the amount of the loan and you were not repaid would you sue the individual?
❑ Yes
❑ No

6.Knowing the risks of non-repayment, would you loan someone you were dating or in a relationship money?
❑ Yes
❑ No

7. Would you co-sign on a bailbond for a person you were dating or in a relationship with?
❑ Yes
❑ No

Pets

Which came first the chicken or the egg? Well as it pertains to pets the majority of singles own some sort of pet; mostly cats and dogs. The down fall to some relationships are some people are allergic to pet hair or just out right don't like them. Now again, the "which came first" philosophy applies?

The pet was there before he /she entered into your life, so should there be a compromise? I have heard several stories in reference to this subject matter. Sometimes the pet won out, meaning the pet owner chose the pet over the relationship. I gained custody of a dog following my divorce. The ironic thing was it was not my dog in the beginning and knew little of the purchase until I got home from work. I once gave the dog as requested as a gift in a relationship; nevertheless, I have the dog to this day. In most cases the pet will always be there for comfort while the pet may be a casualty of the relationship rollercoaster.

Many people have been hit with ultimatums of either it's the pet or them for whatever reasons, maybe insecurity. Ask yourself if the pet wasn't an issue, what next, the minor children? So word to the wise, prior to entering into a relationship let the other know of the understanding or agreement where your pets are concerned and they are a vital part of your family's makeup, so there won't be any conflict down the road. In one case, I heard of a woman getting rid of a dog that was in her family for 7 years before her boyfriend moved in, after he moved in there was an additional conflict and eventually the relationship ended about a month later. Needless to say, her pet was gone. Some issues relating to certain breeds of dogs could be the safety aspect for kids as well as adults.

1.Is having a pet (s) a deal breaker in relationships?
❑ Yes
❑ No

2.Would you end a relationship with him / her if they did not get rid of a pet, after you had requested them to do so?
❑ Yes
❑ No

3. Should one enter into a dating/ relationship knowing that the other person had informed you that he/ she has a pet and is attached to the pet like a family member, but your intentions would be for he/ she to get rid of the animal at a later time?
❑ Yes
❑ No

An Agreed Background Check/ Drug Test

Upon first meeting someone of interest and asking their name, next will come that all important question of marital status. Mine is a little different and goes a little in depth; are you married, have a man, boyfriend, friend or girlfriend. This is an attempt from the beginning to cover all bases. Having been in the investigative field for the past 20 plus years, I have been asked on numerous occasions to inquire of the marital status of someone when they were somewhat skeptical of the individual they were dealing with. The important red flags are often ignored from the very beginning of the relationship, possibly due to the physical appearance and financial indications of the person. I have not performed any background checks in these cases but have provided information on how to perform your own individual background check on a person whether criminal or civil.

What's coincidental is that most women make the best private detectives because they are nosey by nature and can perform their own investigations. I have been privileged to many stories of both men and women dating individuals that were married. So how would one determine if the one you were dating or currently in a relationship was currently married or never quite got their divorce final? It's simple! Hire a detective agency to run a full background and assets check. This could identify any aliases, property, children, criminal and civil history the person may have. Or, be creative, in one scenario a couple, who were going out, seemed to have the same principal in mind when each purchased guns to go on an outing to a gun range. To purchase the guns each had to submit to a background check for the gun purchase. After each National

Crime Investigative Center NCIS check was clear, each party laughed at it later in the relationship. Even though the relationship ended, it was a learning experience for both of them. There will be many times while dating that you will run across married individuals that may not divulge that information. This is where we rationalize due to the physical appearance or financial backing of the individual. If one is whole at the time in their life he or she could possibly recognize this from the beginning. On one occasion, a woman found out that upon the 3 month mark of her marriage that the last name she thought her husband had was not actually his but an alias because he had warrants for many years and changed certain parts of his identity. The way she received the news was from a bails bondsman when she went to post bail for him. There are many instances such as these.

A close friend was in a relationship for almost a year but finally the light bulb came on when she decided to run a property records check within the county her boyfriend had resided and verified that both he and his wife were identified on the deed. Later, she contacted the wife and it was revealed that he had been happily married for 8 years. The lesson here is that there was failure or lack of due diligence in this area which would more than likely result in heartache and great disappointment down the road. As this relates to my own experience, 20 plus years ago, I met a young lady and was curious about a few details in reference to her background, so I asked a friend, who was a military police officer, to run her tag number. The search results not only revealed that she was married but it gave her husband's name and address as well. When I confronted her with this information, there was a reasonable excuse that she left the marriage because he was abusive and that she abandoned all her material items and relocated to another state hoping he would not find her. This actually was the truth, but my issue at the time was this: when you are getting involved with someone, they could also be involving you in some situations that you know nothing about and places you in either danger or an awkward position. So when dating and entering into a relationship at what stage will you chose to have that person interact with your children? Have you done all to protect your children's interest? Some people have been able to hide drug use for months and could be functioning alcoholics and drug users. I have been asked on several instances in opening a conversation with someone and I also make it a practice to ask a person of any prior criminal history and arrest record. Further examinations will have to be used at one's discretion as the relationship progresses.

1.Would you ask someone that you were serious about entering into a relationship with if he/she would submit to a background check and drug test?
❏ Yes
❏ No

2. If it was revealed to you that the person that you were dating or in a relationship with had a history of domestic violence would you continue in the relationship?
❏ Yes
❏ No

3. Would you ask the person that you were in a relationship with their credit score?
❏ Yes
❏ No

The Contract

Agreement on Physical Appearance

(Weight, hair, tattoos, dental hygiene)

Attraction: In general, an attraction draws one object towards another one. The term may have the following specific meaning: the attraction between people which leads to friendships and romantic relationships.

Okay, since we have defined what attraction is, let's acknowledge that in the majority of cases in the initial phases of dating this was the reason the parties connected. So after the dating phase and relationship phase there would be some discussion between the parties of a standard that is to be maintained when it comes to overall general appearance. I have been physically active my entire life and try to maintain a certain physique and weight. Most singles are somewhat required to stay in good physical shape because they are single.

However, when dating or in a relationship, one could get somewhat content and relaxed in the area of weight. Yes, this is a touchy area but not a gray area and for this purpose it should be discussed. In areas such as surgeries, medical ailments, and pregnancies the concerns surrounding one's physical appearance should not be an issue. In the above cases this would be an exception or an agreed upon understanding but not an excuse. The person you are dating or involved with should have an understanding of maintaining the integrity of the appearance of when the two of you first met.

One of the downfalls of relationships is the issue that he/she gained a great amount of weight and from there certain attractions and activities were lost. Should one's agreement as to a certain weight criteria or expectation that is to be maintained (within a certain variance) during the course of the relationship be documented? To take it a step further, should one's dental hygiene be agreed upon within a certain standard as well? How about other changes, such as tattoos or a drastic change in hair styles? Some maybe called shallow for their request for an agreement in this area. But are they? After all, both males and females are very visual beings.

I've heard several discussions from both sides, during the dating relationship phase that a person got comfortable and took the other for granted and let themselves go in physical appearance pertaining to weight. As I have referenced to the pitfalls of dating, it does not mean eating on every occasion. For example: A couple who were meeting for the first time via an internet dating site at a restaurant for the date as one of them approached the table the expression on the others face was priceless, like a thousand words because the person did not truly represent one's accurate depiction in the photo that was online. This information was not updated as information was passed to the other since the initiating of the dating process there was about a 15 pound weight gain. Therefore, if this was a very important factor it should have been identified in the early stages.

We all know the disadvantages of the physical attraction downfall in relationships but I'm focusing on the defined agreement of standards to be discussed and maintained throughout. Some jokes I have heard from both sides of the spectrum is the 5 to 10 pound rule, meaning, if one should exceed that amount and the other shows no attempt to maintain a certain standard he/ she may soon be dismissed. Once I went on a date with a young lady that worked for a dental practice and she required anyone prior to kissing her to either produce documentation of their dental history as it relates to cleaning exams. This may seem a bit extreme, but I'm pointing out some of the dating expectations in these areas. Some elect not to date people with an explicit or great amount of tattoos. This subject matter sparked some questions as it pertained to women and their monthly cycle and why do men avoid you around these time frames of the month.

This could be a key flaw in his character indicating he is not willing to accept you at all times. If he would get ghost or treat one different in actions and activities would this be a deal breaker in the relationship or dating process? In others words, if he's only out for one thing and if he had forehand knowledge he would elect to avoid you as well. What are one's true intentions?If a situation should arise down the road and would this be a test of one's character and define the relationship as the subject matter above.

When I first moved to Atlanta, Georgia in 1992, it was referred to as the" big booty" capital of the world as I would soon find out. As that relates to dating every man was after a so called dime piece but after securing my so called dime, I would find out that it came with a heavy price attached. As most men I was attracted to a nice big butt and a tight waist with the beautiful facial features. The so called Atlanta dream or a total package; however, was not what I expected. I learned this during the course of the dating relationship; I realized that I was not happy with the so called total package. I was with her for about two years. One day the total package arrived at my house and a friend pointed out to me that my whole demeanor changed with her arrival. After realizing this information was accurate and that I was truly unhappy, I learned shortly thereafter that the dream of Atlanta, the total package made me truly unhappy. I had realized that one of the major reasons I was with her is due to her looks and the reactions she received when she entered a room; but the most important of all, I had what every man desired. I was in my mid 20's then and today I am far from that stage and can appreciate a lady's assets from a distance, and know I seek other attributes to go with attractive looks. As that relates to one's appearance I ask when beauty and fineness fades what do you have? I did run into my former total package about 10 years later and let's just say things had truly changed.

1.If the person you were dating or in a relationship with was putting on weight and was less appealing would you continue in the relationship?
❑ Yes
❑ No

2.Would you enter in a dating or relationship if a person had facial tattoos or gold teeth?
❑ Yes
❑ No

3.Do men tend to get (ghost) when a woman is on her monthly cycle?
❑ Yes
❑ No

4.Have you ever run into an ex and he/she had changed drastically, in appearance via weight or other physical attributes?
❑ Yes
❑ No

5.If someone you were dating or in a relationship had bad breath or some other hygiene issue would you bring it to their attention?
❑ Yes
❑ No

6. If the person you were in a relationship with had tattoos of names or faces of their ex would you insist on it being removed?
❑ Yes
❑ No

7. If the person you were in a relationship with had a catastrophic injury would you continue in the relationship?
❑ Yes
❑ No

Ethics and Morals

Ethics: the discipline dealing with what both good and bad in relations to moral duty and obligation. A set moral principles: a theory or system of morals values, the present day materialistic ethic, an old fashion work ethic. This also consists of the principles of conduct governing an individual or a group.

Morals: Of or concerned with the judgment of the good and or bad of human action and character: moral scrutiny; a moral quandary. Teaching or exhibiting the goods or correct nature in character and behavior: Conforming to standards of what is right or just in behavior; virtuous: Arising from conscience or the sense of right and wrong.

Marriage is the ultimate in relationships. Every day you must work 24 hours a day to accomplish one's goals to achieve a successful marriage. A prerequisite to marriage is the process of dating and relationships eventually leading to a committed relationship stage. If you tend to be a slacker and not put the necessary time, commitment and effort to accomplish a successful relationship this may be a result of poor ethics in this person. In a marriage one must work daily to achieve and have a successful marriage which comes with hard work and struggle. Like a job one must have good work ethics as in dating and relationships. Ethics is somewhat of a lost skill. As I have discovered, ethics as well as morals are sometimes forgotten. One's principles, behavior, character, and judgments are lost. I must admit marriage was the best job I've ever had and if God places the challenge in my future, I will gladly accept the responsibility. I have worked several jobs in my life and the more physically demanding the job is the more horrible and down-right lazy work ethics become, I've seen this in a lot of people. Why can't one in the dating process put in the necessary work? As I defined to date or dating, does include seeing more than one person; however, ones ethics and morals should come into the equation when other feelings, emotions, and time is at hand. Some may tend to straddle the fence in actions by using misleading terms during interactions.

Hence, the question is what is one's moral obligation in dating? Should one have good ethics when it comes to others? This is where the term "karma" could affect someone and sometimes guilt of one's actions comes into play.

Some of the feedback that was identified in this area of when you meet one good person how do you decide on which one to date or rationalizing in one's head, are you just having fun, which is what dating is designed to do. Open communication is the key. A question raised here should be if you were to divulge your interactions to the person of interest concerning your actions, or interactions, with others, would it dissolve this relationship? This is where the phrase "it's either feast or famine" relates to dating, when you are in a drought and just as you meet one person another person soon follows. What should one decide? In this area one should try to identify the purpose they have for you or you could be like a silhouette. If the person takes your head of your body a different one could easily be placed with the same expectations that one is seeking. So you shouldn't let these types of individuals who have shown to care so little about you have such an impact and controlling the directions of your life.

Relationships don't come with warranties and one's representative can easily hide the true agenda. This could easily be proven in a simple way- evaluation of every 30 days. Somewhat like a warranty when purchasing a used automobile, at the end of 90 days because a representative can make it this far in dating/ relationships. It's like 90 days same as cash and the last a six month evaluation in a method of 6 months no financing. If there is a one term indication, one would have had time to fully discover true ethics and morals in a wide range of areas. Be sure to ask the right questions and identify any activities and work habits to see if this person that has entered your life is a slacker or not. Otherwise those behaviors may carry over long term to identify their true character and habits? This same could be asked if there were questions of one's home life.

There was a scenario of a married man who said that when he was dating, he would ask to use the bathroom of the lady he was dating. This is to determine her cleanliness as it was a deal breaker for him and would speak volumes about the person and define some of her ethics and morals. His theory was if her bathroom was not to a certain standard or <u>off the chain</u>, he would refrain from further contact or from dating the individual. Now this could go both ways, meaning women practicing this as well. I see both men and women in the gym working out and upon exiting a piece of equipment and they fail to wipe off for the next person. For me this shows no courtesy and this may speak of one's values and ethics. If they show no concern for cleanliness after using equipment is this also a trait that carries over. The hard work that went into the dating process, such as the workout, but one fails to follow through the requirements of the relationship phase as it reflects their neglect in cleaning the machine or equipment. In one instance, he not only concluded the date but didn't feel comfortable in using her facilities.

Some question how he/ she were raised and were there any positive influences in one's child rearing? I can only speak from the male prospective and being the product of a single parent home. I did have the luxury of having several uncles that I would strongly say were good men. In those days it didn't matter of the blood relation you addressed them as aunt and uncle and in return they treated you not as a nephew but as a son or daughter. One of the most positive uncles I had was my Uncle Howard, who walked softly but carried a big stick. Spending a lot of time at his home, I was always being treated as one of his own children. Don't get me wrong, my mother did a hell of a job rearing me but I must admit there is nothing like a man's influence and with my father's absence during my childhood, I missed out on certain areas and subjects that would have aided in my growth as a man. The simple things like changing a tire, fixing things around the house, and learning mechanical duties for vehicles. These things and more could lead to why some women asking where are the real men? For example, if my mother would have discussed me leaving college on a full football scholarship back in 1985, she may have gotten advice to the effect of leave him and let him learn that he's trading football and rigors that go with it for an education. Nevertheless, Uncle Howard wasn't contacted and I was back home and no longer at Albany State College. Just in case you are thinking it… There is NO mama's boy syndrome here! I was too much of a man of the house even back then to be such. As I think back on that experience, this would be the first major occurrence that would change the course of my life. So when I think of real men, I think of my uncle and several friends I have associated with and are active in my life that are single parents as I was after the death of my son's mom in March 1996. My son, the greatest pride and joy of my life, and I were able to continue where his mother had left off when she passed suddenly when he was nine years old.

So many men, such as me, know the daily rigors and sacrifices of women as it relates to rearing children. Without a strong foundation men and women of strong ethics and morals continue on day to day with the demands of trying to manage parenting, dating and hoping to establish a good, healthy and positive relationship so role models could be also defined on both sides of the equation. So when I hear stories such as this one as it relates to morals, ethics, and values that hamper the dating process it causes men to get frustrated.

A male friend I have known for years is career oriented and very successful in his trade, spoke of a situation he was involved in. He explained he was home chilling alone and received a call from a female "friend" that he had prior relations with but again just a "friend." She stated that she was at a local restaurant with her girlfriend having drinks and appetizers and invited him to come through. He stated he would for a quick round. When he arrived he opened a tab and ordered a drink for his friend and himself. After about 30 minutes he closed out his tab and said his goodbyes. While walking down the sidewalk of the establishment he heard a very loud noise of heels running behind him and as his friend approached she stated that he had forgotten to include her tab along with his. Long story short, this was the last time that they interacted and hell no he didn't pay!

1. Is there a grace period when wanting to date friends of the person you were dating or in a relationship with prior?
❑ Yes
❑ No

2. Is having sexual relations on a first date a bad thing or mistake?
❑ Yes
❑ No

3. Should women be more sensitive when ordering food and drink items while dating?
❑ Yes
❑ No

4. Should one consider the role of a man or woman and what type of person they would be in the family structure, prior to dating a person/ relationship?
❑ Yes
❑ No

5. While dating, is it appropriate to ask for any type of financial support whether it is for mortgage, rent, or car to include gas for their vehicle?
❑ Yes
❑ No

6. While on dates, should women order things that they can't afford or wouldn't have ordered if they were paying for?
❑ Yes
❑ No

7.Women have often asked is there is such a thing as a "sexual side of the menu" or a certain price point in which the expectations would require sexual activity at the conclusion of the date?
❑ Yes
❑ No

8.Can a man and woman just be friends without being intimate if there is a strong mutual attraction?
❑ Yes
❑ No

9. Would you tell your mate that his/ her best friend was coming on to you?
❑ Yes
❑ No

10.On a first date, how long should one wait at the destination if you have not heard from the other person?
❑ 30 minutes
❑ 45 minutes
❑ 1 hour

11.This question is for women, is it true upon first meeting a man that you know you will have sex with him?
❑ Yes
❑ No

12.Do women require you display acts of chivalry on dates such as opening of cars doors, pulling out chairs, etc.?
❑ Yes
❑ No

13.If you saw your best friend's man or woman out on a date and it was obvious signs of cheating would you tell him or her?
❑ Yes
❑ No

14. Do you think men look at women differently or less appealing if they have sex while on their cycle?
❑ Yes
❑ No

15. Is it true that women have at least 3 to 4 types of men in their life and call upon each for different requirements?
❑ Yes
❑ No

16. Would men and women dating relationships be rectified or corrected in ways, if both sexes would take corrective measure within their own sex to make each aware of the consequences of their actions?
❑ Yes
❑ No

17. Do men intentionally avoid any type of contact (get ghost) when a woman is on her cycle?
❑ Yes
❑ No

18. Should a man approach a woman to ask her out on a date while she is in the presence of her kids?
❑ Yes
❑ No

19. Should a woman divulge she is on her monthly cycle to a man prior to a date if she suspects that he will initiate sex?
❑ Yes
❑ No

20. Could you date or enter into a relationship with a person who had multiple (at least three) kids by different baby mothers or daddies?
❑ Yes
❑ No

The Contract
142

Why Am I Single?

These were the answers identified
when I asked both men and women the
important question why I am single.

The Contract

Women

• Waiting for the person God has in store for them to complete them.

• Haven't met the right person yet.

• I am single cause I am confident being single.

• Cause I have issues.

• By choice. Not desperate or lonely to the point where I am willing to compromise my wants, needs, and standards in a relationship until the right person comes who desires to fulfill these wants, needs, and standards and I desire to fulfill his.

• I am single because I choose to be. I have plenty of men waiting for me but just not ready to be tied down right now. I have had that long drawn out monogamous relationship before. I just want to have fun without all the requirements of a relationship.

• Cause men do not want to act right.

• In today's society the roles of the men and women have reversed. The men are now more concerned about what a woman has and how much she makes. They are moving into her house and driving her car, but they want to be respected as the man of the house. I'm old school and can't get with the new waive. So until I find a man that want to be the head of my household and not put the emphasis on what I have or don't have, I will be single.

• I'm single because I have been heart broken, emotionless and empty due to the loss of Faith and trust in man. Abused by unbalanced relationships, marriage and dating. Waiting patiently, praying and seeking the companionship, communication and comfort of a Real Man.

• I'm single because after being married two times I need someone who can be a provider, be faithful and give me the attention I need! I can do a lot of things on my own but there are some things a woman need and want from a man.

Men

After repeated requests, no input was received from men that were surveyed.

Synopsis

This brings us to the major question why am I or you single? I've come to the conclusion that one must learn to be comfortable with ones' self being alone, I don't mean comfortable with loneliness, before you can expect another person to enter your life. Over the past couple of years I have undergone several surgeries; including one in 2008, in which I had a cervical fusion on my c3 and c4 vertebrae. I failed to learn the lesson that God had intended for me which was to slow down, be patient and enjoy life.

Some say life is short and enjoy every minute likes it's your last: however, a wrong turn here and there without learning the signs sent to you could make the journey a long one.

Remember a homeless man or woman wasn't born that way when we see them on the street. I think this was the result or at the expense of a bad decision in a relationship? Relationships are an investment of one's time and energy and like the brokerage investment commercial of my youth stated "when E.F. Hutton talks, people listen." This was in reference to investing one's money and we should take the same motto or guidelines in investing one's time. So my defining moment of clarity came Wednesday, 12 January 2011, when I sustained a broken neck in a motor vehicle accident during the Atlanta ice storm. A lot of people questioned how did I actually survive a broken neck and have a very short recovery time? I was blessed from that point on. I've tried to discover God's purpose for sparing my life and believing in the theory that He will not put anyone in my life that was not meant to be there and each will serve their purpose. Also, on that day and months following, God will sometimes remove people from your life to protect you and it is His intent that you let them go. My thoughts are this, if I can share some ideas on dating and relationships that may help or raise dialogue and help close the gap between issues in our community, maybe this was my purpose. As always, I'm still a work in progress but I have learned an entirely new level of communication with women that has identified my strengths and flaws as well as provided insight to others that I have exchanged dialogue with. I've been told I have the gift for gab and I believe I could sit down with the devil and have a conversation even though we can agree to disagree on the subject matter at the very least there was a transaction of communication. Willfully, I welcome God's plans for me with open arms in the dating/relationship arena with the strong belief that He has not spared me to let me falter and He has not brought me this far to leave me. Just as the cartoon character Pig Pen, in Charlie Brown, that walked around with a cloud over his head that everybody around could see you might have to seek how you are perceived through the eyes of your closest friends as I have done. I have learned to be up front first, everybody has flaws and asked yourself if they are willing to support your goals and dreams as you are willing to support theirs.

At this time I would like to apologize to any women I may have mislead, lied to, or manipulated either overtly or covertly in my actions. As I ask for forgiveness, I must forgive my father who never took an active role in my life, but I have come to know him better in recent years. We now communicate quite often. Even though early in my life I only received his name, after realizing his child rearing through communication with my family and his neighbors, I now know he only responded in the ways in which he only knew and that were present to him at the stage in his life and I understand him better today. He was there for me when my family called upon him following my accident. The lesson is I can't ask for forgiveness from others until I can forgive those who have hurt me which makes me the real man I am today. If I can pass down to my son any unsolicited advice about relationships it would be to be patient and not to accept anything less from an individual that expects more of you or that one is willing to give freely. Look for what is in a person's heart for substance and don't just explore the outer surface. These are some of the issues presented to me so I can empower the next generation and wishing him much future success in his parental role with my grandson. I believe timing was the key indicator that all things happen in its due season so when that cloud is removed you will see with clarity that the one you invest your time and energy when one enters your life you will be able to recognize all due to your thought process is complete, meaning one is whole. I have realized that my greatest strength is my greatest weakness and learned how to modify my behavior in matters of the heart and not let my past mishaps dictate my future success. This is what my grandmother spoke of long ago when she said you obtain wisdom through knowledge as our elders have truly seen it all and they also ask the question why? I try not to become set in my ways because change is constant and that agreements may be reached through communication and respect for others' views. Once you have learned to be happy with yourself you won't be in relationships that make you feel less than best/whole.

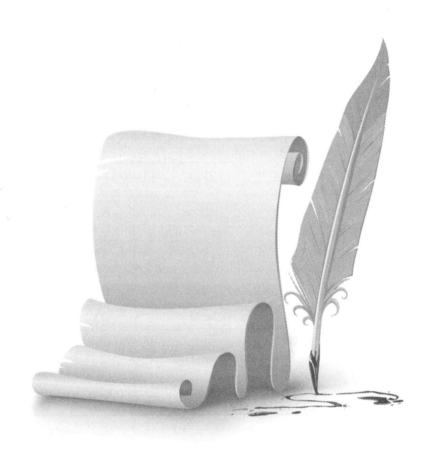

The Contract

Glossary of Terms

90 day-rule- a rule that women have taken hold and used as a measuring stick to see how long a man will continue in the pursuit without throwing in the towel. Its 50% success rate is due to women who fall short and give in to their own desires when sexually aroused.

Adversarial- man vs. woman, pertaining to or characterized by antagonism and conflict.

Affirmation- a positive assertion. A giver or provider, if not careful in dating relationship, will be used and abused due to his or her kindness will be taken as a weakness.

Attraction- draws one's object towards another usually men towards women in the physical sense first, women as well but also require safety, security etc.

Booty call- An after hour appointment for sexual gratification with a person that you have an understanding with but not in a relationship, 90% of the time between the hours after 11 p.m. to 4 a.m., but depending upon each time frame and desires, where each agree to go separate ways with little or no emotional attachment and a sleep over is not the objective or required, sometime arrange via text or phone or after hours from a club, no dating relationship required.

Celibacy- the art of refraining from sex for whatever one's personal reasons.

Cheating- When a person either misleads or deceives another in a relationship by concealing their acts either overtly or covertly so it will not be revealed to the person or persons he or she is currently involved with. Actions could be sexual, inappropriate sexual touching, to include kissing. (If one can't divulge one's actions to the other without consequences and repercussion one has cheated, typical involved in the dating process with the other thinking one is in a relationship or in a relationship, committed relationship or marriage.

Chivalry- or the chivalric code is the traditional code of conduct associated with the medieval institution of knighthood. Over time its meaning has been refined to emphasize more ideals behaviors such as knightly virtues, honor and courtly.

Class- a person of either gender that's cool, calm and collected, carries oneself with dignity, grace, and has reached a full level of maturity, to include dress and language.

Come up- when one achieves something of some type value by surprise and that is usually unearned.

Committed relationship- the stage of a relationship for men right before the grave and a sense of accomplishment for women based upon a mutually agreed-upon commitment involving exclusivity, and agreed-upon behavior.

Communication- with its failure from the onset life will be difficult, is the exchange of thoughts, messages, or information.

Companion- a closely associated "friend"

Contract- what is needed in dating and relationships. A written agreement between two people.

Courtesy- is gentle politeness and manners, is often not shown during first dates which results in it being called a deal breaker is something desired and required from the onset of dating but is often absent.

Courting/Courtship- To endeavor to gain the affections of; to seek in marriage; to woo; to gain favor by attention or flattery to ingratiate one's self with. Courtship sometimes takes the position that there will be no intimate physical contact till marriage.

Cut buddy- this could be a male or female with an unwritten rule that this union is about sex and sex only or commonly referred to as "it's a sex thing."

Daddy's girl- a female with close relationship to her father that is spoiled to the "tee" and expects all men to be of that standard of her father or strive to be such.

Dating down: dating someone that is on a lower caliber as you. Or one who is not excelled as far as you have in any aspect. In the stage you have all but given up at the current time.

Define- to set forth meaning, to explain or identify.

Dog- a guy with no ethics, morals, and standards will say and do what it takes to achieve ones sexual goal.

Dutch- you pay for your items, I'll pay for my items.

Emotions - the feelings associated with the roller coaster ride of dating and relationships are the various bodily feelings associated with mood, temperament, and disposition whether positive or negative.
Equally yoked; 2nd Corinthians 6:14 *Be ye not unequally yoked together with unbelievers: for what fellowship hath righteousness with unrighteousness?*

Ethics-the discipline dealing with what is good and bad and with moral duty and obligation on set principles, this is usually proceeding by one actions of disrespect, not caring and cheating.

Etiquette- this is not practiced by many, both male and female, in today's society; a lost trait, is a code of behavior that delineates expectations for social behavior according to contemporary society and class.

Friend- a person attached to another by feelings of affection or personal regard, a person who gives assistance; a patron; supporter, a person who is on good terms with another, a person who is not hostile "a friend or commonly my friend" is strongly mistaken and out of its proper passage. To put it into proper text as it relates to dating and relationships, a friend is a person who has periodic attachment at certain times, with mixed feelings, which you may or not support depending on certain events and circumstances, and on good terms the majority of times with good understandings. Friend sometimes have a close meaning to the following lingo words like companion, my sponsor, my boo, cut buddy, jump off, freak, home boy/ girl and is associated with the phrases "friends with benefits", "booty call", and the most popular, "we just kicking it".

Funds- cash money, what initiates the dating process.

Gentleman- a man of intellect, well demeanor, polite, sound upbringing; one that you would take home to mama for an introduction of future endeavors in the dating relationship.

Gift- or a present, the transfer of something without the expectation of payment; however if a relationship ends under bad terms it will be converted into a loan if it is money or property and over a certain value; will be in great demand for its return or you will hear about it for the rest of time.

Goal or goals- is a desired end result or final chapter in a relationship; what one sets their initial sights on is a desired result and, plans and commits to achieve a personal or organizational desired.

Good Man- a male that exceeds in manners, standards, etiquette but sometimes loses in the dating relationship process but in the long haul will survive due to the fact that he is in popular demand.

Help mate- Gen 2:18 *And the Lord said it is not good that the man should be alone; I will make him a help meet for him.*

Honesty – the forgotten trait in the dating relationship process refers to one's moral character such as integrity, truthfulness, and straight-forwardness along with the absence of lying, cheating, or theft.

Hypocrite - Someone who practices hypocrisy, which pretends to hold beliefs or whose actions are not consistent with their claimed beliefs. Usually a man but not in all cases; one who can't take what he can dish out.

In the meantime- a person or persons you elect to invest your time in with no expectation of happiness (until you can identify a different point of attack.)

Independent woman- A woman who pays her way to include bills; depends on a man for nada; one who is on a strong foundation and exudes confidence but is usually without a man or relationship.

Infidelity- unfaithfulness, to one that you are in a relationship of a serious nature with   when there was an understanding of no others involved. See cheating (Page 116).

Insane-expecting the person you are in love with to finally act right, the craziness or madness of behaviors, staying in the relationship leaving and returning and getting the same result.

Integrity- this concept had been inconsistent within the dating arena in recent time. It is a concept of consistency of actions, values, principles, expectations, and outcomes. In ethics, integrity is regarded as the honesty.

Investment- All money, time, and energy given to the relationship.

Kickin it- chillen; nothing serious See "friend" (page 118).

Lady- a female of high social class or status: elegant, kind, and good hearted moved with grace and elegance.

Lingo- is a form of speech; commonly words of slang of street/ ghetto origin.

Loan- something that is usually not returned or paid back; usually money or property.

Love- an emotion of strong affection and personal attachment; a virtue representing kindness and compassion and affection.

Lust – often confused or associated with love. It is a strong physical attraction for another person, generally sexual in nature.

Mama's boy- A grown man who is heavily influenced in his decision by his mama or grandmother; who is weak and can't stand alone; his mother is usually involved in every aspect of his life, his relationships, job, career.

Meet and greet- a pre stage of a date to determine if there is any type of attraction to require an actual date; commonly used on dating internet sites or a blind date.

Morals- the judgment of the good or bad in human action and character: in the dating and relationship phase this is the first to go, along with ethics as the steps of cheating occur.

Needs- If either party in a relationship DOES NOT have these met, you bet each will be seeking elsewhere to have these fulfilled. It is something that is necessary for organisms to live.

Old school – (and older era in time could be music, thought process, clothes, and cars but respected due its place and standing in time.)

Picky- over rationalizing everything to include a mate; usually occurs when one still fails to realize they don't know actually what they want even if it's right in front of them.

Politics- generally applied to the art of science but as it relates to dating the conflicts that continue to mount with no clear indication of a resolution long term.

Quality time- commonly referred to as (QT), often what is demanded in relationships but was actually started as time spent with love ones, family, partners, that was productive, profitable, but most importantly, it was special time specifically set aside for activities in which attention was undivided.
61.Real man- There is a myth that these individuals do not exist. However, unlike Bigfoot, they are everywhere: One who loves God, well rounded, responsible, good morals, and values, He is a man of his word, trustworthy, secure with himself, financially able to take care of his responsibility and provide for his family.

Relationship - a connection, association, or involvement between persons by blood or marriage, an emotional or another connection between people, an involvement or sexual affair.

Religion- is a collection of cultural systems, beliefs, and worldwide views that relate humanity to spirituality and sometimes, to moral values. In most cases in relationships if you don't have religion or at least a spiritual foundation or attend church you are lost and will be at the curb of the church.

Representative- both male and female; the person that typically shows up on the first date and may continue to the 90 day mark to impress the opposite sex.

Respect- this is said to be earned? If not given, freely during dating and relationships stages; gives a positive feeling of esteem or deference for a person and specific actions and conduct.

Selfish- only thinking of one's own interest and having no regard for others usually follows with action of disrespect.

Serial dater- a man or woman who dates obsessively over and over with no clear purpose other than to conquer something that is lacking with oneself; this person hampers and causes controversy in the dating practice and makes it difficult for more mature and serious minded individuals. If it is a man, usually a player, with means but not always and seeking sex. If it's a woman, she's seeking a free meal and occasional sex depending on if the man does not mess up and say the wrong thing. Serial daters usually don't remember you; only bits of conversation or what eating establishment they were at as a reference for remembrance.

Set in one ways- one who is not subject to change, budge, even with no thought in the matter.

Spoiled- When one expects the world centers around them and all their wants and needs should be satisfied by someone other than them.

Sponsor- a man, the majority of time, that pays for all aspects of dating usually with the intent of having sexual relations at the conclusion of the outing. This person may pay bills, mortgage, rent, in the hope of future endeavors of sex, sometimes confused with the old school version of a sugar daddy.

Standards- this all often lowered in dating and relationship arena due to shortage of the opposite sex; was often thought to be a norm or convention.

Submit: to give over or yield to the authority of another; subject to some kind of treatment or influence; to present for the approval, consideration, or decision of another or others.

Temptation- the desire to perform an action that one may enjoy immediately or in the short term but will probably later regret for various reasons: usually alcohol is involved; not on all occasions and one thinks you won't get caught.

Timing- is the control of time of speed of action or event so it can occur at the proper moment.

Trick- a term used to described a woman that misleads a man where finances and sex are largely involved. The end result is usually a man's money is exhausted and she is no longer around.

Values- a lost art or tradition that was thought to be a principle or foundation that measures integrity.

Wants – confused 75% of the time with the word needs, as associated to women is closely relates to her desires.

The Contract

DATING RELATIONSHIP
Contract

The Contract is made on _____
between Party One _____
and Party Two _____
City of _____ State of _____

The parties agree to renew the contact on a
month to month basis or go their separate ways.

These parties agree to the stipulations as follow:

1. Marriage?
Party One (man) agrees to
❑ Yes
❑ No
   Party Two (female) agrees to
❑ Yes
❑ No
If yes what time frame _____
Desired Ring cost $_____
If the engagement should end, the ring is to be returned to _____.
Party One ❑ Yes ❑ No
Party Two❑ Yes ❑ No

2. Kids?
Party One
❑ Yes
❑ No

Party Two
❑ Yes
❑ No
   If yes time frame _____

3. Living Arrangements?
Party One agrees to stipulation ❑ Yes ❑ No
Party Two agrees to stipulation ❑ Yes ❑ No
Stipulation for section three as follows:
a) Party One agrees to pay for all living expenses within household
b) Party One agrees to pay for mortgage or rent with Party Two pays all other expenses
c) Party One and Party Two mutual agree to split cost ½
d) Party One and Party Two agrees to mutually the divide cost by the number of occupants within the
house hold with the custodial parent for children or adults of blood relation assuming the cost for each where in.

4. Dating Phase:
Party One agrees to stipulation ❏ Yes ❏ No
Party Two agrees to stipulation ❏ Yes ❏ No
Stipulation for the section as follows:
a) Party One agrees to pay for all dates
b) Party One agrees to pay for ½ dates
c) Party One agrees to pay for ¾ dates

Dating others:
Party One agrees to stipulation ❏ Yes ❏ No
Party Two agrees to stipulation ❏ Yes ❏ No
Stipulation as follows:
a) Party One and Party Two agree only see one another
b) Party One and Party Two agree to see others in dating process

Activities per week:
Stipulations are as follows:
Party One agrees to stipulation Party Two agrees to stipulation
a)Party one and two agree to see each ___ times a week in agreed upon activities.
Party One Initial _____
Party Two Initials _____
    Sexual activity:
a) Party One and Party -Two agree to sexual activity _____ times a week.
Party One Initials _____
Party Two Initials _____

5.Parties agree to keep family and friends out of the personal aspects of the relationships.
Party One ❏ Yes ❏ No
Party Two ❏ Yes ❏ No

6. Church:
a) Parties attend church services together.
b) Parties attend church services apart.
        Party One ❏ Yes ❏ No
        Party Two ❏ Yes ❏ No

7. Background Check/ Drug Test:
a) Parties agree to testing
b) Parties do not agree
        Party One ❏ Yes ❏ No
        Party Two ❏ Yes ❏ No
8. Physical Testing/ HIV:
a) Parties agree to testing
b) Parties do not agree to testing
        Party One ❏ Yes ❏ No
        Party Two ❏ Yes ❏ No
9. Pets:
a) Parties agree to no pets
b) Parties agree to have pets
        Party One ❏ Yes ❏ No
        Party Two ❏ Yes ❏ No

5. Loans and Gifts

a) Parties agree to stipulate that funds over$ __ will be a loan.

b) Any monies given by either party is looked as a gift.

     Party One ❑ Yes ❑ No

     Party Two ❑ Yes ❑ No

6. Physical Appearance

a) Parties both agree to maintain agreed upon weight standards

b) Parties agree to no more than a ____lbs weight gain for each partner.

     Party One ❑ Yes ❑ No

     Party Two ❑ Yes ❑ No

7. Income, Credit, and Divorce Decree Documentation

a) Parties agree to provide documents for line 12 of contract.

b) Parties agree to refrain from showing documents.

     Party One ❑ Yes ❑ No

     Party Two ❑ Yes ❑ No

Signatures:

Party One _____

Party Two _____

Date: _____